China Doll
Clinton, Gore and the
Selling of the U. S. Presidency

Originally published, in booklet form, as
"What Red China Got for its Money
Why did the People's Republic of China invest
in the 1996 Reelection Campaign of
President Bill Clinton?"

By
Roger Canfield, Ph.D.
and
Richard A. Delgaudio

Published by United States Intelligence Council 2000

The United States Intelligence Council is incorporated under the IRS code as a 501(c) 4 corporation. The United States Intelligence Council researches intelligence information important to the security, economic, national defense and independent sovereign interests of the United States, and disseminates this information to interested American citizens.

The Council encourages citizens to regularly communicate with their U.S. Senators and their Congressman on these issues. For inquiry to your U.S. Senator or U.S. Congressman, you may telephone the Capitol Switchboard, (202) 225-3121.

For those interested in accessing additional information about our elected officials via the Internet,

U.S. Senate Internet Home Page http://www.senate.gov, and U.S. House of Representatives Internet Home page http://www.house.gov.

To communicate with Senators and Representatives by mail:

Honorable (name of Senator)
United States Senate
Washington, DC 20510-2203
Salutation "Dear Senator (name):"

Honorable (name of Representative)
United States House of Representatives
Washington, DC 20515-1101
Salutation "Dear Congressman (name):"

Please write to your two U.S. Senators and to your Representative concerning the matters raised in this publication. We also strongly encourage you to support the work of United States Intelligence Council, including continued distribution of this publication and others like it, by sending your donation (not tax deductible) to:

United States Intelligence Council
P.O. Box 98018
Washington, DC 20090

Cover design by Paul D'Innocenzo;front cover art by John Connors.

*Dedicated to the freedom of our children
Blaine, Carlton, Alicia, Kara, Jason, and Lee.
And grandchildren Jeremy and Jacob.*

And to the courageous civil servants whose dedication to the truth damaged their safe careers as bureaucrats, but may have saved their country — Notra Trulock, former security director of the Department of Energy (DOE) and Charles La Bella, former Justice Department prosecutor. Others who paid dearly for their testimony before Congress or for their professional integrity are: Edward McCallum of DOE; Jon Fox, Michael Maloof, and Peter M. Loiter of the Department of Defense; Roberta Parker, Daniel Wehr, Kevin Sheridan, and Ivian C. Smith of the FBI.

United States Intelligence Council

Dr. Roger Canfield is executive director of the U.S. Intelligence Council. A respected political analyst, he served as a public policy consultant for the California legislature from 1980-2000. Roger is a former daily political columnist for the *Sacramento Union* and former host of a political radio program. His articles have been published in *Military, Human Events, National Review, New American, Dispatches* and many newspapers. He received the "Medal of Patriotic Commander" from the families and survivors of the Nicaragua Resistance in honor of his assistance in the liberation of the Nicaraguan people from Communist rule. He earned a Ph.D. in Government from the Claremont Graduate School and published his dissertation as *Black Ghetto Riots and Campus Disorders.* He has studied and taught international relations and is a Navy veteran. Roger lives with his wife Noel in Sacramento, California. They are proud parents of three children and two grandchildren.

Richard A. Delgaudio, who serves as the U.S. Intelligence Council's chairman of the board, is president of the National Security Center and the Legal Affairs Council. A leader in conservative causes for more than 30 years, he has made numerous TV and radio talk show appearances. Richard is the author of the book, *Peril in Panama,* and the forthcoming *Still a Just Cause.* A participant in five fact-finding missions to Panama and a sponsor of five others, he recently presented testimony to Congress on the issue of Communist Chinese interests in the Panama Canal. He is a former Senior National Director of Young Americans for Freedom and, later, YAF Alumni Chairman and National Advisory Board Member. A devoted father, Richard enjoys skiing, scuba diving and taking Tae Kwon Do with his three children.

Table of Contents

Introduction

Red China is now waging a "secret war" against America. In the early 21st Century the Communist rulers of China will command a modern military with nuclear weapons "on a par with the United States," according to a unanimous secret bipartisan report of Congress headed by Rep. Christopher Cox. For six months Bill Clinton delayed release of the Cox report and dribbled out pieces of it so slowly that once it was released it was a dull thud — rather than a shocking revelation of political cover-up, obstruction, betrayal and treason. Chalk up another "victory" for the spin doctors, and sadly, a defeat for America.

Meanwhile America will have no defenses against the nuclear missiles stolen and/or given to the Red Chinese. Our citizens are unaware of these perils because our own president, William Jefferson Clinton, has lied to us about the dangers of nuclear annihilation. Further, he has lied about the trustworthiness of treaties with the Chinese Communists, their influence upon our elections, the secret military technology he has given them and the Chinese theft of 50 years of American nuclear secrets. Testimony before Congress has revealed that his Attorney General Janet Reno has systematically delayed, covered-up and obstructed investigations of blatant Red Chinese espionage and illegal campaign funding of one American political party.

The Clinton administration and its friends in the Democrat Party — in particular Senator John Glenn and Rep. Henry Waxman — together with the media, obstructed the investigation by the Thompson committee of illegal foreign political contributions. More than 120 persons fled the country or pled the Fifth Amendment. They flat-out refused to testify about Red Chinese interference in the 1996 elections. Clinton-friendly judges doled out small fines and community service to Chinese-Americans who carried the cash, but refused to reveal much about either the Red Chinese and their American business friends giving cash or the Clinton agents and allies accepting it.

Many inside the beltway and near the Rotunda of the Capitol are aware of these matters. And many Americans surely recall bits and pieces of this information.

But since the Congress has not been shaken by any earthquakes, no massive and sweeping indictments have taken place, no major change in policy, no massive overhaul and change in U.S. - Communist China policy has occurred, this book being published in an election year can perform a vital and important service for the democratic process.

Are the American people happy with what Congress has done in the past two years, or would they prefer stronger oversight and legislation?

If the American people understood the facts as summarized in this book, would they demand Congress act to hold the Executive Branch accountable?

Should more be done to counteract Communist China's participation in U.S. elections?

This book gives the American people the whole picture without Clintonite spin-doctor wizardry, sneaky machinations and smoke-shrouded maneuvers.

This book proves that Bill Clinton gave away or allowed the Communist Chinese to steal every military device they need — including nuclear missile technology — to threaten the destruction of the United States of America. Every citizen concerned with Bill Clinton's willingness to sacrifice U.S. national security in exchange for an illusive "strategic partnership" with the emerging nuclear world power Red China will want to read this book.

The President who replaces Bill Clinton will inherit an American policy of appeasing Red China with whatever it wants at the expense of our national security. As in the past, this appeasement has failed to satisfy Communist China, which is anxious to exercise its power in world affairs. Thanks to Bill Clinton, China 2000 will have more accurate, more numerous and more deadly nuclear weapons than ever before in its history. Thanks to Bill Clinton, Communist China will have what he simply calls a more "modernized" military. Will this "modernized" Communist Chinese military be credited to the man whose policies helped make it all possible, Bill Clinton? Will the American people come to understand why our children face a greater threat in the future than they did in the past — Bill Clinton? They will if this book receives widespread distribution.

China Doll presents a graven image of a President darkly influenced by the Communists who still rule mainland China by brute force and exercise influence in American elections through campaign cash given directly and by their American business partners, along with old fashioned espionage, rarely countered and almost never punished. If that seems too harsh read on.

This is a short book, a simple book about something fundamental — the survival of our great nation.

As a California state legislator, I am especially alarmed by the interference of Communist China and its American allies in the U.S. election process. This insidious undermining of the sovereignty of our country strikes at the root of American democracy and self-determination. So far, the interference in our election process has not been thwarted, it has not been punished, and it has not been diminished. As this book documents, such interference seems to have paid off handsomely in a pro-Red China policy by the U.S. I pray that widespread distribution of this book will change this policy and end Communist China's interference in our elections and counter growing nuclear missile threat.

The informed reader will be aware of many of the events described in this book, but you will appreciate how the authors have tied together most of the great national security scandals of the Clinton administration.

I wish every American has the opportunity to read this book and to understand the perils that this nation's national security now face from Communist China and will continue to face in the post-Clinton era.

Through the generous contributions of average

Americans and the miracle of modern printing technologies, the United States Intelligence Council has set for itself the ambitious goal of distributing one million copies of this book.

I hope you can help accomplish that goal by reading this book, buying others, and passing them on to fellow Americans. I especially hope you can help by asking your Senators and your Congressman to read this book and to do something to thwart both Communist China's future interference in America's election process and that nation's threat to our country using stolen nuclear missile technology.

God Bless you.

Hon. Steve Baldwin
California State Assemblyman

Assemblyman Steve Baldwin (R) is a former Executive Director of Young Americans for Freedom, and Co-Chairman of the June 2000 Long Beach Summit on the Red China Threat to the U.S.A. organized by U.S. Intelligence Council

Chapter 1

Red China's Nuclear Threat: Designed in the USA, Made in China

"President Clinton is solely responsible...we are totally defenseless against an incoming ICBM from China..."

Senator James Inhofe, R-Oklahoma,
floor of the U.S. Senate, March 15, 1999.

The United States is not now at war with the Peoples Republic of China (PRC) Yet China is on a secret warfooting building nuclear missiles at a rapid rate, "modernizing" its armed forces. If we go to war — as the country China calls its "main enemy" since the Tiananmen Square Massacre — innocent citizens of the USA as well as American soldiers, sailors, and marines may pay with their lives for Clinton's aiding and abetting of Red Chinese nuclear espionage. Under a last strike nuclear missile attack, American civilization or some millions of her citizens might be vaporized — removed from the face of the earth just as a long for- gotten world power named Carthage was once oblit- erated by Rome. Today America has no missile defenses whatsoever against nuclear missiles made in China, but designed in the USA. Americans and our allies defending U.S. interests overseas also are totally vulnerable to the nuclear, chemical, and biological missiles, which Red China has helped Iran, Iraq, Syria, Pakistan and North Korea develop. A world of "madmen and missiles."

And William Jefferson Clinton is the one man most responsible for the danger of nuclear blackmail or nuclear horror. Clinton and his political allies in the Congress and his political appointees in the bureaucracy continue to lie about the need to protect Americans from these dangers. The consequence of lying about dangers to one's countrymen may be fatal or severely harmful. The Cox report and the Thompson report reveal that the Red Chinese stole, bought, or were given American military technology and bought access and political influence with campaign cash. The Chinese are today using improved missile guidance systems given to them by Loral and Hughes Corporations. On August 2, 1999 the Chinese successfully test-fired a long-range missile, the Dong Feng (East Wind)-31. [East Wind Rain was the Japanese code for an attack on Pearl Harbor]. The DF-31 uses a stolen or Clinton supplied American warhead, solid rocket engine, reentry nose cone and guidance designs.

Reds have stolen, designed, built, and tested miniature nuclear warheads (W-88) necessary for multiple target missiles, mobile missiles, and submarine launched missiles. The road mobile DF-31 with a miniature warhead can be deployed to reach any target in America. China was expected to test-fire the Julang (Big Wave) 2, a submarine launched multiple-warhead missile with a range of 8,100 miles in late 1999. They have stolen, built and tested neutron bomb warheads that irradiate people, but save property. After months of denials, in July 1999 China admitted it had both neutron and miniature nuclear warheads, but claimed they were not stolen. At the 78th anniversary of the founding of the Communist party on June 30, 1999 President Jiang Zemin proclaimed that "socialism will triumph over capitalism." At the Fiftieth Anniversary celebration of the Communist conquest of China on October 1, 1999, the Chinese bragged about shooting down 890 US aircraft in Korea, Vietnam, and China and paraded their new JL-2 sub missile and DF-31 mobile missile in Tiananmen Square. These missiles require the miniature nuclear warheads China stole from us. The Red Chinese have begun to deploy these nuclear warheads. They did not wait the ten years the Clinton administration expected.

Clinton's reckless disregard for national security and his insatiable appetite for political campaign cash will shortly make America more vulnerable to a nuclear missile attack than during the Cold War. The Red Chinese bluster about attacks on Los Angeles during the 1996 confrontation in the Straits of Taiwan or its 1999 threat to hit US carriers off Taiwan are not entirely empty bluffs. They can take out Taiwan, Los Angeles, or an aircraft carrier. This is unlikely — as were attacks upon the Maine, the

Lusitania, Pearl Harbor, South Korea, Kuwait.

Improved missile guidance — now deployed — given to the Red Chinese by Clinton's major corporate campaign contributors at the Loral and Hughes corporations (Bernard Schwartz and Michael Armstrong respectively) enables the Chinese to accurately target their missiles within yards of any target in America. Adding multiple miniature warheads (W-88 design) stolen from American nuclear labs at Los Alamos, New Mexico (built and tested by China and paraded in Tiananmen), the possible targets become hundreds of cities in 49 states. The previous 24 one-warhead Chinese missiles rise in multiples of three to 10 warheads per missile to a possible 60-200 on the 20 new Loral and Hughes improved guidance missiles, DF-31s, deployed in 1999. Once the Communist Chinese pick up control of the ports and bases of the Panama Canal (as originally reported by co-author Richard Delgaudio of the National Security Center and admitted by Clinton in early December 1999) former chairman of the U.S. Joint Chiefs of Staff, retired Admiral Thomas Moorer, recently warned that China could launch a nuclear attack on the U. S. The southern half of Florida and the southeast USA would be vulnerable to short-range and intermediate range nuclear missiles. American miniature W-88 warheads will make multiple warheads possible on a single missile and make lighter weight missiles mobile. Missiles made mobile are very difficult to detect upon waterways, roads, railways, and submarines. Making those warheads neutron bombs — the stolen, built, and tested W-70 warhead — will let the Chinese irradiate the American people and leave our wealth and property intact. Red Chinese stolen, built, and tested warhead designs are "on a par" with America's. That's horrible. There's more.

Thanks to Bill Clinton's intentional giveaway (export waivers) of improved missile launch and guidance, fiber optic and encrypted telecommunications, military-industrial machine tools, lasers, and supercomputers we are a lot less safe on his watch than in the administrations of Presidents Carter, Reagan, and Bush.

Because of Clinton's blind eye to the Chinese proliferation of missile guidance and other components of weapons of mass destruction, we and allies such as Taiwan, Japan, Korea and Israel, will be increasingly open — as never before — to missile attack from Iran, Syria, Libya, North Korea. Bill Clinton told lies to appease and to protect his illegal campaign contributors, both domestic and foreign. Protecting the business interests of his American campaign contributors and appeasing the militarism of his illegal Red Chinese government contributors, William Jefferson Clinton has threatened our survival.

Clinton lied and covered up his relations with the Red Chinese government, their collaborators, and their spies. The Cox report and others reveal the missile guidance, supercomputers, telecommunications and other technologies that the Clinton administration sold directly to the People's Liberation Army (PLA) or its military operations and intelligence officers.

Clinton's reckless disregard for national security allowed the Chinese to steal fifty years of nuclear weapons, seven warheads, and millions of lines of computer "legacy" codes, models, and data which stripped naked America's once secret warhead designs. Floating in cyberspace, this technology can be resold in international commerce. During 1998 and early 1999, at least five hackers penetrated the insecure computer systems at the nuclear weapons labs. Secrets reside on desktop computers and floppy discs which a China testing cyberwar may have violated.

The Clinton administration lied and covered up. Clinton political appointees in the Department of Energy, National Security Council, and the Department of Justice consistently used the plausible "spin," lawyer's technicality, or useful lie of the day. They fought the discovery of the truth, delayed investigations, protected suspected spies, controlled political damage, and covered up the dangerous consequences of the Clinton China policy. Once the Red Chinese espionage became known to scores of top Clinton administration officials — for nearly four years they covered up weapons thefts, refused to tighten security, retaliated against whistleblowers, investigators, and professional civil servants, and obstructed internal and FBI investigations. Incompetently or treasonously, Attorney General Janet Reno, her Deputy Eric Holder, and other Justice Department attorneys misapplied the lack of "probable cause" — appropriate to shoplifting — to the theft of nuclear secrets threatening millions of lives. They protected the "civil rights" of a suspected spy — Wen Ho Lee — from FBI wiretaps, house searches, computer searches, polygraphs, and interviews. The delay allowed him to download fifty years of America's nuclear secrets. For over three years they denied and delayed the discovery of truths embarrassing to themselves and to their Chinese "strategic partners," but possibly fatal to their countrymen. President Clinton disregarded scores of internal government reports from many sources including the FBI, CIA, GAO, and Congressional Committees. Then in November 1998, the Clinton administration was definitely informed in a secret report that Clinton had himself commissioned, that China posed an "acute [and continuing] intelligence threat" to nuclear weapons labs.

There was no reasonable doubt — the espionage was real and ongoing.

Plausible deniability was gone - everybody knew.

There was no way to blame Ronald Reagan or the Republicans. Fifteen of sixteen thefts were discovered on the Clinton watch. All of the cover-ups and all of the lies were on the Clinton watch.

So what did the Clintonistas do?

They first gave Wen Ho Lee (and others?) another five months to try to delete the evidence from his computer. They lied. They covered up. They blamed Ronald Reagan and the Republicans. They played the "race card" alleging that suspecting any Chinese person was evidence of an investigation motivated by racism.

And finally they appointed their own Rudman Commission and two internal Inspector General reports at the Departments of Energy and Justice. Clinton and his political appointees were white washed and air brushed out of the picture. They now blamed the FBI investigators and DOE and other bureaucrats. It was a contemptuous attack on career civil servants some of whom had risked their jobs to tell the truth.

Chapter 2

Appeasing and Protecting
Red China

Remember Clinton's campaign slogan "It's the economy, stupid"? Our response to China policy hurting U.S. national security is that "character counts."

Like many ego-inflated politicians Bill Clinton thinks he knows the ways of the world. He charms his way through the day. He feels our pain. He tells most of us what we want to hear most of the time. He's a liar. He's successful. He thinks he can get away with it. Most of the time he does.

Clinton gets women. He gets power. He gets his way. He's President. He beats his Republican foes. Whatever his moral limitations — everyone on the planet knows them — he's a winner. He's smarter than just about anybody on Earth. Not admirable, but he's worldly in a way that tough leaders have to be. And that's why a majority of Americans did not want him impeached over lying or even obstructing justice — about sex. Clinton's lies are no longer about sex and dirty politics. The bipartisan Cox report detailing Chinese espionage was adopted unanimously. The national security consequences of Chinese espionage and Clinton's loose security and trade policies are not questionable. Between every cold, dull line of the bi-partisan Cox report can be read lines of Clinton lies. On every page facts directly contradict the public words and deeds of the President and of all the President's men — and women.

Character counts. Clinton is a serial liar, a pathological liar — a self-absorbed person, a sociopath. He lies to himself. Clinton's flaws are harmful to his country, perhaps fatal in the future. Politicians are often guilty of delusions of their own superior intelligence, charm and powers of persuasion. Such self-delusions too often spill the blood and waste treasure of the peoples it is their solemn obligation to protect. Bill Clinton has placed our nation in great peril. And a new President may not be able to fix it on time.

The Charms of Appeasement

Like British Prime Minister Neville Chamberlain meeting Adolph Hitler in Munich in 1938 — Clinton has met his match. Hitler's secret war aims (after the Rhineland, Austria) did not stop with the British appeasement of the fabricated grievances of the ethnic Germans in Czechoslovakia. Nor is Clinton's appeasement of the Chinese working to stop the Chinese secret war against the "main enemy" — the USA. The Chinese build their military machine for war — designed in the USA — and they threaten war over Taiwan. They threaten to neutron bomb any US carrier close to Taiwan. They bluster over mere mention of American theatre missile defenses for U.S. soldiers. From Tiananmen to Tarawa the Chinese are giving nothing back. They are emboldened. They laughed at Clinton's human rights whimper before the UN Human Rights Commission. They smirked as Clinton gave his TV lecture on democracy in Beijing in July 1998. As for Chinese espionage, Premier Zhu Rongji joked — he offered to paint "Made in China" on his missiles. He asked for "clues" so he could help American investigators. The Chinese sent a General who had threatened to incinerate Los Angeles to visit Clinton in the White House. Clinton groveled endlessly over the accidental US bombing of the Red Chinese Embassy in Belgrade. The Communists laid siege to the American Embassy in Beijing. They lied. They screamed. They insulted. The more Clinton appeased the Communists the more contemptuous of America and the more threatening they became.

Like President Roosevelt at Yalta with Communist butcher Joseph Stalin in 1945 — Clinton has met his match. Territorial concessions in Poland did not fill Stalin's appetite for East Germany, Hungary, Romania, Czechoslovakia, Yugoslavia, Bulgaria. Nor will Clinton's territorial concessions to the Chinese be enough to appease the Chinese. They will not be placated with a free missile shot or two at Free China on Taiwan. They now have or will soon have: a naval station on Tarawa; Chinese controlled Hutchinson-Whampoa company operated ports, bases and facilities at the Panama Canal; PLA owned China Ocean Shipping Company (COSCO) control of the Long Beach Naval Station (or the equivalent space in Long Beach or in Los Angeles); a naval base on the Spratly Islands; or a 8,000 foot runway on the Paracel Islands. They won't be satisfied. Clinton's territorial appeasements will not fulfill Red Chinese appetites. They wanted more — Clinton gave them satellite photos of Okinawa and who knows what else. Like President Nixon and his arrogant foreign policy advisor Professor Henry Kissinger in Hanoi in 1972 (and like Al Haig — now a consultant to the Red Chinese) Clinton has met his match. Communist troops and weapons did not stay in place after the treaty signing in Paris in 1973. And Red China's solemn paper promises not to transfer nuclear, chemical, biological, computer or other technologies to other countries are being violated every day. In late July of 1999 Bill Gertz of the Washington Times reported continued Chinese missile shipments to North Korea. North Korea buys and sells missile components and fuels from the Sudan, Syria, Pakistan, Egypt, Iran, and Libya. Indeed, the Chinese and the Koreans have ignored each and every freshly signed security agreement with Clinton.

Clinton fawns over the Chinese Premier and President. He fights for permanent normal (Most Favored Nation) trade status for Chinese. In the face of opposition of 75% of Americans according to an October Zogby poll, on November 15, 1999 Clinton approved a trade deal that he said earned the

Chinese membership into the World Trade Organization (WTO).

No matter what the Chinese do Clinton and his emissaries have beaten a well trod path to kneel again and again to beg the Red Chinese, begging for a "strategic partnership" of engagement and trade — a relationship that China actually has with Russia. The Clintonistas claim this "strategic partnership" is the true road to peace, prosperity, and democracy in China. Taiwan has 30,000 companies and $60 billion invested in China and cannot appease the Communists, but Clinton thinks otherwise.

No evidence to the contrary will dissuade the Clinton team from their course of appeasement:

Nothing.

Not Chinese conversion of "civilian" technology — supercomputer, communications, satellite guidance — to military uses. Not the indictment of McDonnell Douglas for its sale of aircraft machine tools to China for military use. Not seven stolen nuclear warheads. Not sales of missiles or nuclear weapons to Pakistan, Iran, Syria, Libya, North Korea. Not missiles fired over Taiwan. Nor Japan. Neither executions of political prisoners nor forced abortions of girl babies. Not threats of incinerating Los Angeles or vaporizing aircraft carriers. Not missiles putting millions of Americans in peril. Not GAO reports, CIA reports, not the Thompson and the Cox reports. Not even the *New York Times*.

Nothing.

Appeasement — more trade.

As shocking news of Chinese espionage came to public light in the spring of 1999 William Jefferson Clinton warmly greeted Chinese Premier Zhu Ronghi in Washington to negotiate Chinese membership in the WTO. WTO membership would be the equivalent of an open checkbook from American investors and international bankers. It would also mean permanent normal (Most Favored Nation) trade relations status to America's enemy and foe in the next century.

It was quite a spectacle.

On April 7 Chinese Premier Zhu Rongji arrived for happy talk with President Clinton who warned U.S. politicians to avoid a "campaign-driven Cold War" with Beijing. Clinton wanted "principled, purposeful engagement" and to avoid turning the world's most populous country into an enemy. Cold War would have "tragic consequences: an America riven by mistrust and bitter accusations, an end to diplomatic contacts that have produced tangible gains for our people, a climate of mistrust that hurts Chinese Americans and undermines the exchanges that are opening China to the world," he said. Echoes of 70 years of futile trade with the Evil Soviet Empire.

Strange coming from Clinton, who in 1992 had accused President George Bush, of "coddling tyrants in Beijing" by sending visitors to China.

Republican presidential candidate Steve Forbes

said that that Zhu's visit "will be another episode of Clinton-Gore appeasement of China."

Forced by the spring espionage scandals to possibly delay final action on the WTO, Clinton sent Commerce Secretary William Daley to China to warn Beijing about "anti-Chinese" sentiment. Clinton declared that U.S. restrictions on exports to China "are tougher than those applied to any other major exporting country in the world."

Bill Triplett, co-author of *Year of the Rat,* and *Red Dragon Rising* told Ramesh Chandran of the Times of India, "I was open-mouthed.... [T]his is probably the most shameless, fraudulent, political speech in the last ten years." It was another Clinton lie. A whopper. For a few million in campaign funds from China and its corporate sponsors Clinton had thrown away 50 years of export control rules and hemorrhaged the lifeblood of his nation's national security technology.

Into late May 1999 — whatever the revelations of Beijing's perfidy or Clinton's cover-ups — Clinton was still bent on trading America's security and freedom for shiploads of beanie babies, walnuts, oranges and cheap textiles. Clinton's minions still championed Chinese entry into the WTO.

No longer would China's behavior on human rights or the proliferation of weapons of mass destruction be used to restrict trade. Certainly no nuclear espionage coups.

Responding to every Chinese threat to pull out of

WTO negotiations, Clinton rushed to complete by June a breath-taking package of new trade agreements with China. An hour before Zhu's departure, U.S. Trade Rep. Charlene Barcshefsky met with Wu Yi at his Willard Hotel room at 3 a.m. Until 7 a.m. she begged him to buy American wheat, oranges, and chickens in return for US "strongly supporting WTO entry."

All of this to get cheap Chinese goods produced with slave, child, and prison labor. Clinton, the accomplished American politician, knew that every new vision of an American commodity or service sold to the mythical "1.2 billion Chinese" (earning $260 a year) also purchased new domestic American political constituencies for Clinton's China policies.

So like a panting pacifist in heat, Clinton trade negotiator Robert Cassidy beat Zhu Rongji back to China to continue the nonstop trade "negotiations." Through pleading the possible trade agreements began to accumulate — wheat, citrus, chickens, banking, insurance, telecommunications, software, civil aviation, perhaps textiles and services. Shamelessly unstated the 1.2 billion Chinese also might provide subsistence labor — even slave labor — for American industries such as textiles, steel, electronics. Reuters reported unnamed "business leaders...criticized the White House for...bowing to politics."

Columnist Georgie Anne Geyer said: "...[American] companies... have become lobbyists for China." William Hawkins in the *Weekly Standard*, said, "firms with investments in or trade ties...lobby Washington to appease the regimes. Change is dangerous for those who have become collaborators." Clinton — ever the political master in domestic affairs — was building a formidable coalition in favor of his China policy. Top CEOs of US corporations attended the 78th anniversary of the founding of the Communist party. By November 1999 the U.S. Chamber of Commerce urged China's ascent to the WTO. However, off the water's edge, Clinton was still playing a dangerous game of which he was not the master. Quite the contrary. The Chinese have made him their China Doll — a toy for Red Chinese geopolitical advances.

As William Hawkins said in the *Weekly Standard*, "firms...seek to protect their interests. They lobby Washington to appease the regimes. Change is dangerous for those who have become collaborators."

After Zhu's tour, the Clinton administration complained about human rights in China. The Chinese showed utter contempt. "Beijing thumbed its nose at Washington the Saturday after the UN Commission on Human Rights shelved a U.S. resolution criticizing China's human rights record," one news service wrote. It was an "anti-China farce," said PRC Foreign Ministry spokesman

Sun Yuxi. China's envoy Qiao Zonghuai said the complaint was "totally groundless. ...The United States keeps nagging China over trials of a few criminals in China's judiciary," Qiao said. Within months China would jail 35,000.

Fast forward to November 15, 1999 Clinton concluded 13 years of talks on a trade deal with China on telecommunications, entertainment, and financial and insurance services. China made no concessions on proliferation of weapons of mass destruction. China made no concessions on child, slave, or prison labor. China would gain increased access to US high technology and the U.S. institutions would finance it. Clinton declared China qualified for the WTO. Reform Party presidential candidate Patrick J. Buchanan said, "The deal that was cut in Beijing was a complete capitulation... In return, we got nothing in the way of human rights improvement, nothing in the way that would build-down the missiles aimed at Taiwan, nothing in the way of reduced belligerence to this country." Only in 2000 could Congress stop expanded Chinese access to trade by refusing China permanent normal trade relations. Once given WTO status China's trade would be outside the jurisdiction of any U.S. law.

Chapter 3

Clinton Lies: Proliferation and Missile Defenses

> *"It is my understanding that the investigation
> has not yet determined for sure that
> espionage occurred. ...
> No one has reported to me that they suspect
> [any espionage since his presidency began]."*
> William Jefferson Clinton,
> press conference, March 19, 1999.

Clinton is unconcerned about Chinese proliferation of weapons of mass destruction to potential American enemies such as Iran, Syria, North Korea and Libya. Red Chinese theft of fifty years of American secrets about nuclear weapons does not seem to worry this President.

Long after most Americans stopped caring about Clinton lying about sex and his private life, Clinton continued to lie about matters of much greater national importance — national security and national survival. The two wars in Yugoslavia to stop genocide and attacks on a Somalian aspirin factory and an Afghan tent camp to stop terrorism have shown the American people that Bill Clinton will lie about things more serious to statecraft than sex — genocide and terrorism.

• He lied about the Chinese proliferation of weapons of mass destruction to American enemies and his knowledge of those weapons transfers.

• He lied about Chinese espionage and his knowledge of espionage.

• He lied about Chinese conversion of "civilian" technology to military uses and his direct actions to facilitate exports of such technology.

• He lied about the safety of the American people from nuclear missile attack.

Clinton lies about Chinese proliferation of weapons of mass destruction

Clinton repeatedly lied about Red Chinese proliferation of weapons of mass destruction to Iran, Pakistan, and North Korea. In April 1999, as Johnny Chung's ties to Chinese military intelligence and Chinese thefts of the neutron bomb both became public for the first time, Clinton lied about problems with the Chinese being reported to him by US intelligence services. Afterall, the Chinese were trustworthy. "I think if we hadn't been working with China, China would not have signed the Comprehensive Test Ban Treaty, the Chemical Weapons Convention; they would very likely not have refrained from transferring dangerous technology and weaponry to countries that we don't believe should get it."

Clinton denied the truth of proliferation rather than admit he was refusing to obey the law. China's proliferation of weapons of mass destruction required him to continue to restrict trade with China.

Clinton had practice lying about this subject since at least 1997. Though the PLA owned Great Wall Industries had been cited by American government agencies for missile sales to Pakistan and Iran, Clinton granted militarily useful waivers to Loral for satellite sales and to Tandem for supercomputer sales to the proven proliferator China's Great Wall Industries.

On the eve of the arrival of Chinese President Jiang Zemin to tour the U.S., Jon Fox of the Defense Special Weapons Agency was ordered to rewrite his own memo that China was a proliferator to say that China was a nonproliferator. In late October 1997 as Chinese President Jiang Zemin toured the U.S., Clinton looked on, never raising the issue of Chinese proliferation.

• A U.S. intelligence report had just revealed that China had built a plant in Iran making equipment for the production of chemical weapons. Also aircraft and missiles.

• On January 21, 1998, Clinton falsely certified to the U.S. Congress that China was "not assisting ...any non-nuclear-weapons state...in acquiring nuclear explosive devices." In secret testimony before the Senate Foreign Relations Committee, civil servant Robert Einhorn revealed that China was assisting Iran and Pakistan.

• According to a secret memo of March 12, 1998 by Gary Samore, a White House NSC aide, the Clinton administration planned a great missile deal for the Communists. In return [for yet another] Chinese promise to [again] stop sending missile technology to Iran, Libya and Pakistan — for such a useless pledge — Clinton was willing, indeed eager to "expedite...U.S. [missile] exports to China."

• In late December 1998, the Cox Commission cited Clinton's failure to hold China to account for sales of weapons of mass destruction to Iran and Pakistan.

• Clinton received the classified Cox report and continued to lie about Chinese proliferation while Chinese premier Zhu Rongji toured the USA in April 1999.

Bad news did not disrupt the Clintonistas' head-long rush to improved relations, trade, and give-aways. There was the happy visit of President Jiang Zemin in October 1997, the "strategic partnership." declared by President Clinton on his visit to Beijing in July 1998, Premier Zhu Rongji's WTO negotia-tions and tour in April 1999, Clinton's phony lecture on democracy to a radio-less Chinese people in Beijing in July 1999, and the signing of a WTO opening trade deal on November 15, 1999. In 1999 the cocksure Reds held celebrations of the founding of the Communist party and of the Communist conquest of China and paraded their weapons.

On March 15, 1999, Sen. James Inhofe, R-Oklahoma, said that Clinton intentionally lied 130 times from 1995 through 1997 about missiles targeted at America. Clinton persisted in telling one of his favorites — 130 times:

"For the first time since the dawn of the nuclear age, there is not a single solitary nuclear missile pointed at an American child tonight. Not one. Not a single one."

By lying to the American people about their safety, Clinton gave new meaning to the "Big Lie" that Hitler said made the best propaganda.

• Clinton systematically dismantled the Reagan Strategic Defense Initiative, which had swept the Evil Empire into the dustbin of history.

• Clinton knew that China had nuclear-tipped ICBMs targeted at the US. And yet he signed export control waivers allowing transfer of improved rocket launches of satellites (missile guidance) to China.

• Clinton vetoed Republican missile defense legislation in 1995, and in 1999 he delayed deployment after he was forced to sign missile defense legislation.

• Against the advice of his own Secretaries of State and Defense, Clinton loosened export controls on missile technology by moving approvals out of Defense and State Departments into the pro-trade Commerce Department. At the Pentagon's Defense Threat Agency, Michael Maloof opposed easy technology transfers to China because of its security threat to the U.S.

• Maloof says he is "isolated, ignored and subject to political retribution" for his views.

• After release of the Cox Report, Congress returned export controls to the Pentagon, but there Clinton appointee John Hambre rushed to defang the legislation.

• Hambre moved export licensing into an office dealing with export-favoring defense contractors and out of a defense policy office concerned with proliferation.

• On December 16, 1999 the office — was given only two days to veto an export — made a rubber stamp of Clinton and Chinese policy.

• By August 2000 Hambre plans to move the Defense Threat Reduction Agency to an Army base far from the Pentagon and other interested agencies.

• Clinton did not object to the North Koreans firing missiles into the Japanese and Alaskan airspace. Nor did he tell the American people that China fired missiles into Taiwan airspace in March 1996, simulated missile firings in 1998, and expanded its missile batteries targeted at Taiwan in 1999 to 100.

• Clinton is unconcerned that any mention of

missile defense of America or its Asian allies angers the Chinese. China is incensed by American proposals for a Theater Missile Defense for American troops in Asia.

• American talk of a missile umbrella over 50-year U.S. ally Taiwan makes Red China furious and it threatens "serious consequences."

• The Chinese are angry that missile defenses just might make Chinese nuclear missiles worthless. Major General Yang Huan, Chinese deputy commander of the Strategic Rocket Forces in a 1989 article indicated his fear of American "Star Wars" defense.

• In April 1999 Clinton's Secretary of State, Madeleine Albright flew to Beijing to calm the Chinese — not to worry, the US will not have missile defenses for a decade, she said.

• Clinton had put missile defenses in his 1999 budget, but conditioned deployment upon the improbable — a Russian agreement to scrap the ABM treaty.

• Clinton officials have argued that missile defenses are not ready for deployment. The Theater High Altitude Area Defense anti-missile system failed six test launches. Senate Foreign Relations committee chairman Jesse Helms notes that all of the "failures" were "quality control problems" — a bent connector, a loose wire, a nozzle rupture. None had anything to do with the hit-to-kill technology.

Concluding that "failures" prove a national missile defense is impossible is like asserting that "a flat tire on an airplane proves that man cannot fly."

• On May 6, 1999 the Chinese yet again responded negatively to a U.S. Defense Department report submitted to Congress citing China's missile buildup facing Taiwan as a reason for including Taiwan in an Asian missile shield. Selling Taiwan missile defenses...would be "severe interference in China's internal affairs...." Zhu said.

• "I believe the Chinese and the American people can learn from one another...Actually there is a lot we can learn from each other." Chinese Premier Zhu Rongji, Libertyville, Illinois, April 11, 1999.

• In mid June and early August 1999 after intensive quality control measures, the U.S. twice successfully shoots down a missile 50 miles away in the upper atmosphere and in space with the Army's Theatre High Altitude Area Defense (THAAD) interceptor. The small, light interceptor detects, tracks, and "Hits to Kill" without an explosive. The Clinton administration delays a deployment decision until June 2000.

• After a successful Chinese test of its DF-31 long-range missile and Chinese transfers of missile parts to North Korea, China pressed its case against Taiwan defenses — E-2 electronic warfare aircraft and F-16 parts. James Moriarty, one U.S. Embassy official among others, joins the Red opposition.

(*Washington Times* August 3, 1999).

• Speaking at his office overlooking Pearl Harbor, on November 12, 1999 Adm. Dennis Blair, commander in chief of the U.S. Pacific Command, said, "I think we need a theatre missile defense to protect the troops [and Japan and South Korea] ...within range of North Korean [missiles]...." He favors helping Taiwan build missile defenses against China's 500 to 600 missiles.

• The Admiral claims China is aware the U.S. would defend Taiwan. The question is whether the Chinese believe the Admiral or the Clintonistas panting to please them.

• In late November State Department spokesman James Rubin said that the U.S. does "not preclude the sale of theatre missile-defense systems to Taiwan," and denies that the State Department agreed with China in opposing such defenses. Rubin insists it is "premature" to discuss specific systems and opposes Congress actually requiring missile defenses for Taiwan. Clintonesque.

• Pentagon officials tell Gertz of the *Washington Times* that senior White House and State Department officials are resisting providing Taiwan with advanced Patriot or Army and Navy theatre missile defenses. Rubin calls such claims "wildly inaccurate."

Time has long passed for William Jefferson

Clinton to tell the truth about American missile defenses and to stop delaying deployment of tested technologies.

Chapter 4

The Cover-Up:
Nuclear Espionage

During one critical moment in the congressional hearings in 1974 over the burglary of the DNC headquarters at the Watergate Hotel in July 1972 Sen. Howard Baker asked a critical question. "What did the President know and when did he know it?" This chapter answers that question for William Jefferson Clinton.

What follows is a month-by-month and sometimes day-by-day chronology. In summary, the Chinese were caught stealing nuclear secrets in 1994 on the Clinton watch, but Clinton did nothing significant to improve security until late 1998, covered up the loss, in order to develop a "strategic" relationship with the Chinese.

In 1989 Maj. Gen. Yang Huan, deputy commander of China's Strategic Rocket Forces, set three goals for China's strategic nuclear weapons: to improve their survivability, striking ability, and penetration (of defenses).

In 1993 the Department of Energy (DOE) eliminates color-coded security badges at nuclear labs as "discriminatory" and drops FBI background checks for lab workers and visitors.

In 1994 both Commerce Secretary Ron Brown and DOE Secretary Hazel O'Leary allegedly sell seats on trade missions to China for $50,000-$100,00 each. Paid or free, Brown and O'Leary are accompanied on these missions by PLA pals Johnny Chung, John Huang, Charlie Trie, and Loral chairman Bernard Schwartz.

In an October 1994 trip to Beijing U.S. Defense Secretary William Perry promises Gen. Ding Henggao, head of COSTIND, a "Cray computer to be used by the Chinese nuclear weapons establishment to help design newer and safer nukes." (Smith, April 27, 1999).

Prior to a DOE trade mission to China in February 1995, DOE O'Leary waives background checks for foreign scientists visiting nuclear weapons labs. Thereafter 1,500 Chinese scientists and military intelligence officers wander through the labs without security and escorts. 10,000 pages of classified documents disappear from one facility.

In the February 1995 trade mission, O'Leary met the head of China National Nuclear Corporation right after loosening nuclear lab security. Johnny Chung is an "unofficial delegate" on the O'Leary trade mission and a friend of officers of the PLA such as Lt. Col. Liu Chaoying, a Communist, high-tech spy and arms broker. Chung is a major conduit for illegal Red Chinese contributors (via intelligence officers Lt. Col. Liu Chaoying and PLA military intelligence chief, General Ji Shengde) to Clinton, and a 57-time visitor to the White House.

O'Leary dismissively crosses out a SECRET classification on a drawing of a W-87 nuclear warhead and gives it back to a *US News & World Report* reporter who publishes it on July 31, 1995.

In 1995 Clinton issues an executive order to declassify 1.6 billion pages of documents — by April 2000 — classified material over 25 years old. Some nuclear designs are declassified.

American nuclear scientists give lectures in Beijing. Wen Ho Lee goes there twice and publicly embraces a Red Chinese visitor to Los Alamos.

Mostly from 1994-1995 Lee transfers 1,000 files of warhead codes from a classified computer to his desktop computer — accessible to outsiders. In 1998-99 alone five hackers access lab system.

The Clintonistas consider open access to nuclear information "engagement" with China. The thefts of neutron bomb designs coincided with both DOE O'Leary's relaxation of lab security and "trade" missions to China in February 1995.

Receiving campaign cash from the Red Chinese and their US corporate trade partners, Clinton fawns over Red Chinese visitors to the White House in 1994-99.

In April 1995 the U.S. detects Chinese nuclear test patterns similar to U.S. tests on W-88 warhead. Robert Henson, a physicist, informs DOE security chief Notra Trulock of the loss of the W-88 design. Theft is likely. The damage is great. A miniaturized warhead equals MIRVs, mobile, and sub missiles.

In June 1995 a "walk in" gives the CIA Chinese documents containing design secrets of the W-88 miniaturized nuclear warhead. Paul Redmond, the

CIA's former chief of counterintelligence, who caught Soviet mole Aldrich Ames, calls the theft of miniaturized W-88, "far more damaging to the national security than...Ames."

In July and November 1995 the CIA Director John Deutsch informs the Clinton administration — Chief of Staff Leon Panetta and then Presidential NSC advisor Anthony Lake — of the thefts according to multiple unnamed sources in the *New York Times* confirmed by White House spokesman Jim Kennedy and the Rudman report. (June 27-28, 1999).

In October 1995 DOE fires whistleblower Robert Henson, 61, in a staff cut but hires 30 others.

In late 1995-early 1996 Trulock briefs FBI on 12 suspects (nine Caucasians). By February 1996 the FBI and DOE narrow to five suspects — one is Wen Ho Lee. Managers at the Los Alamos nuclear lab want to access Lee's computer, but DOJ lawyers fear a search will taint evidence.

By early 1996 a Red Chinese official brags to an American spy about the recent 1995 theft of the design for a neutron bomb. Trulock briefs Paul Redmond at CIA; "This is going to be as bad as the Rosenbergs," who were executed for giving atomic bomb secrets to the Soviet Union.

In April 1996 Trulock briefs White House NSC Director Sandy Berger that the Chinese stole the W-88 miniaturized warhead and the neutron bomb design.

By July 1996 the DOE believes both the W-88 and neutron bomb thefts may involve the same suspect and Wen Ho Lee is on a short list.

June 1996, the FBI opens formal investigation into W-88 theft.

Fearing congressional actions against Clinton China policy, acting DOE chief Elizabeth Moler and new DOE Secretary Frederico Pena choose to downplay and cover up the nuclear thefts for three years.

In early 1997 Pena puts counterintelligence on "back burner" for a year. Trulock waits four months to report new evidence of spy operations to a Pena unavailable to his own security chief. "Beginning in early 1997, senior DOE officials...urged me to cover up and bury this case. For months these officials refused to authorize intelligence to brief...Secretary Frederico Pena..." says Trulock.

"Twice in 1997, the director of the FBI urged DOE senior officials, including Secretary Pena and Deputy Secretary Moler, that FBI investigations should not prevent DOE from taking immediate action to protect sensitive information," says Trulock.

"And yet for another 14 months...these suspects continued to retain their clearances and accesses..."

April, 1997 DOE refuses FBI request to reinstitute background checks for lab visitors (eliminated nearly three years earlier in 1994). Congress learns of "thousands of foreign visitors," Background checks are ignored for another 17 months

In the spring of 1997 prime spy suspect Lee is chosen to run a sensitive new nuclear weapons program.

"... In the middle of 1997...[began]...a pattern of

harassment, intimidation, and retaliation...continued over the next two years," Trulock later recalls.

FBI Director Louis Freeh told Moler, in July 1997 that the investigation would not be hurt if Lee's security clearance was lifted or if he was transferred to a less sensitive job. But Moler does not pass the information to John Browne at Los Alamos.

In July 1997 Trulock gives NSC's Berger a detailed briefing on "China's full access," Berger briefs Clinton on W-88, lab security, neutron bomb theft, CIA and FBI both warn Pena of lax security.

In August 1997 Trulock briefs a disbelieving Gary Samore at NSC in the White House. Samore immediately requests quick, narrowly focused, alternative CIA analysis. Also in August 1997 Berger flies to Beijing to plan for October meeting of Jiang and Clinton.

Clinton-Jiang discussions include an agreement to ease exports of commercial nuclear technology.

On October 24, 1997 a Pentagon arms control officer, Jonathan Fox, is ordered by the White House to say that the transfer of information about handling fissionable nuclear fuels is "not inimical (harmful) to the common defense or security of the United States." Fox drops his true view that it would "present real and substantial risks," when his job is threatened.

In November 1997, the redease of a third Inspector General's report results in the demotion of Trulock as head of DOE security.

By the fall of 1997 the FBI learns suspect Wen Ho Lee has traveled to Shanghai, China. FBI alerts the

White House, and asks the Department of Justice to apply to a special court for a wiretap under the Foreign Intelligence Surveillance Act. Acting Director of the Office, Gerald Schroeder, and his assistant, Alan Kornblum, tell the FBI they do not have enough evidence and refuse to apply. The FBI goes over Schroeder's head to Deputy Attorney General Eric Holder. Holder refuses their request for a wiretap. Attorney General Janet Reno, who has refused an Independent Counsel to look into Red Chinese political contributions to Clinton, likewise concurs in her deputies' refusals to request a wiretap.

While the Justice Department refuses only one or two of 1,100 foreign intelligence wiretaps each year, it denied four separate requests from the FBI. This one has "embarrassed" China.

Having no wiretap, the FBI does not have enough evidence to arrest their prime suspect.

Wen Ho Lee keeps his security clearance until September 1998 and his job until March 8, 1999.

In September of 1997, Gary Samore tells Berger that the CIA report is "less conclusive about the extent of the damage" than DOE's report. Berger and Samore continue planning to build a "strategic partnership" with China while the CIA report was only minor differences, the Clinton administration continues to assert to the press that it clears them.

From late 1997 to February 1998, Clinton orders new counterintelligence measures – nearly three years after discovery of the theft of W-88. Clinton's order to allegedly reestablish tighter lab security (Presidential Decision Directive 61) is dated February 1998. Yet Wen Ho Lee remains in place with his security clearance and computer access – transferring data from a secure computer into one accessed by a simple password. (Later Lee says three passwords).

In July of 1998 Pena/Moler at DOE order Trulock not to brief the House Intelligence Committee. Moler fears Congress will attack Clinton China policy. Trulock's testimony is limited to lab visitors, but the issue of thefts comes up. Trulock does "not respond fully" to the Committee.

In October 1998 Moler orders Trulock to limit his testimony to foreign visitors to the nuclear labs, but denies gagging Trulock about nuclear thefts before the House National Security Committee.

The General Accounting Office concludes in 1998 report that the labs used background checks on only one to two percent of visitors from China or Russia, left data unguarded in hallways, and let unescorted visitors roam 24 hours a day.

In the Fall of 1998 Trulock briefs incoming DOE Secretary Bill Richardson who orders background checks and doubles counterintelligence budget. Richardson urges Berger to coordinate testimony before Cox Committee. Berger assigns disbeliever Samore to "coordinate." Richardson is tough on security, but downplays damage and Clinton responsibility.

In November 1998 Clinton receives a secret report that China presents "an acute intelligence threat" to the nuclear weapons labs and that the lab's computers are constantly penetrated.

In late 1998 Trulock secretly testifies before the Cox Committee about the theft of neutron bomb and W-88 technology.

Rep. Norm Dicks, D-Wash., tells Secretary Richardson he is unhappy with Clinton delay and inaction. Berger swears under oath to Cox Committee that Clinton was not told about nuclear thefts until 1998 — directly contradicting Trulock and other corroborating witnesses in the *New York Times*. In fact, Berger had briefed Clinton in July of 1997, and others, such as Leon Panetta and Tony Lake, as early as 1995. Everybody in the security business knew about a historic case of espionage — the DOE, CIA FBI, NSC, Clinton Chief of Staff. Why not Clinton?

"Our assessments came under [direct] attack only after we provided testimony to the House Cox-Dicks panel in the fall of 1998," remembers Trulock.

In December 1998 the summary of the classified Cox report and the circumspect Cox news release only indicate that Chinese actions — both the political influence and the thefts — "harmed national security" without providing any significant details.

Suspect Lee is given a polygraph, a lie detector, in February 1999. Lee fails test: "Have you ever given nuclear secrets to an unauthorized person?"

Unknown to FBI, within two days Lee tries deleting records to hide his previous transfers of nuclear data to his own insecure computer. In two months, early April, Wen Ho Lee's office computer is searched and his deletions restored. Lee will have deleted more than 1,000 top-secret files of computer codes to hide their improper transfer. "An individual is suspected of being a spy with access to all of our warhead information ... and we did not get into his computer. "Total incompetence," Sen. Don Nickles, R-Okla., said.

Vice President Gore, who takes full credit for the Internet, Love Story and Love Canal, denies any responsibility: Calls the nuclear espionage a problem "that happened during the previous administration and the law enforcement agencies have pressed it and pursued it aggressively with our full support." Secretary Richardson says, "there's no evidence of any more [espionage] cases" at the weapons labs. It is doubtful that both Gore and Richardson are ignorant of the neutron bomb theft on Clinton watch revealed to them by both Trulock and by the still classified Cox report.

March 8, 1999 the DOE fires Wen Ho Lee — three years after he became a prime suspect.

March 9, 10, 12, 1999. The denials and cover-ups thicken. "It is absolutely not true that we downplayed evidence of this," says State Department spokesman James Rubin. White House spokesman Joe Lockhart says the administration launched "a vigorous assessment using the CIA and other assets in our national security operation." NSC advisor Gary Sampore – who had asked for a quick second opinion to save the fall 1997 summit with the Chinese and had fought to reduce export controls on missile technology — says, "The idea that we tried to cover up or downplay...to limit damage to U.S.-Chinese relations is absolutely wrong."

March 10, 1999. Berger, who had been first briefed by Trulock in April 1996 — nearly three years previously — declares, "I reject the notion there was any dragging of feet." James Brooks writes that Wen Ho Lee's neighbors find him a friendly and generous fellow who shares his plums and Peking duck.

On March 12, 1999 Clinton — his Chief of Staff and NSC briefed in July and November 1995 four years previously, himself briefed in July 1997 nearly two years previously and slow to restore and enforce lab security — said, "We did not ignore evidence. Quite the contrary; we acted on it."

March 15, 1999 Berger admits the Chinese "benefited" from leaks of nuclear information.

March 19, 1999 Clinton says, "Our efforts to have an honest and open policy with China...has paid dividends." Clinton cites signing of treaties with China on chemical weapons, nuclear tests.

Answering a question on March 19, 1999, President Clinton says, "It is my understanding that the investigation has not yet determined for sure that espionage occurred."

Clinton appoints Rep. Jane Harman to the Foreign Intelligence Advisory Board to review security threats at the nuclear labs. Harman's prior law practice included representing the People's Republic of China, registered as a foreign agent. Clinton also appoints former Senator Warren Rudman as chairman of the ad hoc group. Rudman promises a "hard hitting report," but William Safire predicts a "whitewash."

Edward McCallum of DOE Security tells the Rudman Commission that the DOE has a "long history of suppression and reprisal" of those disclosing security breaches. Three days after McCallum talks to the Commission he is accused of a security breach, put on administrative leave, but is not prosecuted.

On March 15, Lee admits contacts with Red China's scientists, intelligence and law enforcement officers.

On March 27, 1999 the FBI interviews Lee. The FBI discovers that Lee had used a large magnetic tape drive to improperly transfer nearly 2,000 classified computer files from 1983-1995. The files contain millions of lines of code describing programs and data derived from hundreds of underground nuclear-weapons tests and simulations. The test information is contained in an insecure lab computer accessible to outsiders. For the nearly three years he had been a prime suspect in the theft of the W-88 warhead, Lee used his computer. Clinton claims he is not informed about Lee until March 31, 1999.

April 7, 1999 — at least a week after discovering Lee's file transfers — the DOE finally halts all lab computers "over fears that security lapses make the computers vulnerable to espionage..."

April 8, 1999 the *New York Times* publicly reveals that the designs of the neutron bomb were stolen in

1995, that Berger was briefed in April 1996, and Clinton was briefed in July 1997. This is not just another case of decades-long espionage at the nuclear labs — this one was discovered and then systematically covered up during the Clinton administration.

Clinton and Zhu respond

Washington rolled out the red carpet for Chinese Premier Zhu Rongji, guest of honor at a black-tie White House dinner, supping on roasted salmon, kumquat tartlets and mango pudding and listening to a recital by cellist Yo-Yo Ma.

As Clinton's special guest Zhu is ready. Zhu says: "I have no knowledge whatsoever of any allegation of espionage or the theft of nuclear technology and I do not believe such stories...I've also asked President Jiang, and he does not have any knowledge...It is not the policy of China to steal so-called military secrets from the United States."

Clinton says, "I can only say that America is a big country with a big government and occasionally things happen in this government that I don't know about. ...So I think it's important that we continue the investigation... and I asked for his cooperation."

Zhu said he would cooperate with American investigators as long as the United States provided some clues for China to follow up.

China had already demonstrated what it did with "clues." For several years the PRC refused Justice Department and congressional access to financial records of campaign transactions or to fleeing witnesses. It refused visas for all investigators. And it refused to extradite subpoenaed suspects to testify.

On April 10, 1999 the FBI searches Wen Ho Lee's home 10 days after the discovery of his transfers of millions of lines computer programs and data.

On April 12 and 15 Notra Trulock testifies before the House Armed Services Committee detailing widespread resistance to his investigations. Before the Senate Armed Services Committee on April 12, 1999 Trulock says, "our warnings were ignored...they were minimized and occasionally ridiculed....Over four years we briefed over 50 senior officials...We briefed the National Security Council, Mr. Berger, twice; we briefed other members of the NSC. We briefed the Secretary of Defense and his staffs. We briefed CIA Director Tenet, before him [CIA] Director Deutsch; Director of the FBI; the Attorney General [Janet Reno], the Secretary of State."

On April 17, 1999 DOE Secretary Richardson restarts nuclear lab computers after a 10-day shutdown – presumably because any problem is solved.

In mid-April 1999 Zhu tours U.S. with Clinton bemoaning "anti-Chinese rhetoric" and warning of a "new Cold War." The White House blames Gary Samore for inaccurate briefing of Berger, not mentioning Trulock's briefings of Berger himself.

Trulock's Truth: Vindication

In late April an independent CIA report — not a

Samore/Berger term paper — confirms Trulock's conclusions, a senior intelligence official said. "We expect that future Chinese weapons will look more like ours," said the unnamed official. CIA Director George Tenet briefs congressional intelligence committees on the CIA's assessment of China's acquisition of U.S. nuclear secrets. A set of unclassified key findings says that China obtained at least basic design information on several U.S. nuclear weapons including the Trident II W88 miniaturized nuclear warhead. China also obtained information on a variety of U.S. weapon design concepts and features including the neutron bomb, the report said.

On April 28 1999 the *New York Times* reveals that mostly in 1994 and 1995 — "On Clinton's watch" — Lee transferred millions of lines of computer code and warhead performance data. The computer code covering fifty years of nuclear research — "legacy" code or the "crown jewels" — may have compromised "virtually every nuclear weapon in the United States arsenal." Ray E. Kidder, a nuclear physicist at Lawrence Livermore Laboratory, describes the data as the equivalent of a scientific blueprint. "If you've got the source code and the input data, you can reverse engineer the thing and have a complete plan for (the) nuclear explosive part of the weapon," he says. The data may have "spilled out all over the world" says William Safire. Rep. Christopher Cox says, "China is the number one proliferator. Now secrets are out there in the stream of commerce, and probably on to Iran and North Korea and Libya." Strategically, nations like Japan, South Korea, India, Russia, Israel might have much to fear from their soon-to-be- nuclear foes.

On April 29, 1999 Richardson says, "This is serious, but it does not constitute a compromise of any strong magnitude."

April 30, 1999 labs establish for the first time a means to scan lab computers and E-mail for outgoing classified material — five years after Wen Ho Lee makes millions of lines of classified computer files accessible to the outside world.

On May 2, 1999 the *New York Times* reveals that Clinton had been warned by a secret report in November 1998 that China was an "acute intelligence threat" to nuclear labs and that computer systems at the labs were being constantly penetrated.

The Senate Intelligence Committee on May 5, 1999, calls for a moratorium on foreign scientific exchanges at the weapons labs and boosts spending by $30 million to protect the labs' computer systems.

After six months of Clinton delays in declassifying the Cox Report and Clinton dribbling out the contents, the Cox Report is released on May 25, 1999. It lands with an anti-climatic thud. Everyone is tired.

Clinton spokesman Joe Lockhart responds to the Cox report saying, "If you're looking at this Presidency, I can't point to a case where we know something was stolen, we know who did it and we know where it went and we know where it came from." Not on our watch. Not us. Not the Chinese. Nothing happened.

Out of town, Clinton says, "I strongly believe that our continuing engagement with China has produced benefits for our national security." Full speed ahead. The testimony of Trulock and reports in the New York Times and the Los Angeles Times lead straight away to one and only one conclusion — Clinton knew about the nuclear thefts and covered them up. His DOE refused to brief the House Intelligence Committee. Neither chairman of the Intelligence Committees in the Senate nor House was ever briefed on an espionage coup that is equal to the delivery of secrets of the first atom bombs to Moscow by Julius and Ethel Rosenberg, who were executed for their treason against their country. "The very people...who resisted, minimized, delayed, and ultimately blocked our efforts to reform are now in charge of implementing the fixes," testified Notra Trulock before the Senate Armed Services Committee in April 1999.

"I think heads should roll," said Sen. Don Nickles R-Okla. Yet William Clinton was considering appointing Elizabeth Moler as Secretary of the Air Force.

On May 28, 1999 Richardson awards Trulock $10,000 for his contributions to national security, but Trulock does not get his job back.

On June 9, 1999 Ed Curran, DOE Chief of Counterintelligence drops a bombshell claiming that the [Republican] Senate knew about Chinese spying in 1996 and had done nothing about it. Democrat

Senator Bob Kerry, D-Nebraska, rises to call such claims "inaccurate and too partisan...It carried a tone ...written by the political shop at the White House." Under fire Secretary Richardson also admits that Curran's comments and facts were wrong. FBI agents complained of "deliberate incompetence" at the Department of Justice. Down for the count, the Clinton administration rebounds with a counteroffensive. They go on the attack.

In June the Presidential Foreign Intelligence Advisory Board (the Rudman Commission) releases its report. On first glance it is a scathing indictment of the DOE whose bad security record is blamed upon "organizational disarray, managerial neglect, and a culture of arrogance...[which] conspired to create an espionage scandal waiting to happen." Nasty. Mean. "The DOE is a dysfunctional bureaucracy...incapable of reforming itself." True. The shift of blame. The bureaucrats did it. In six weeks a bipartisan Senate would pass a reorganization bill putting the nuclear labs under a new Agency for Nuclear Stewardship. Sen. John Warner, R-Virginia, assures everyone that the reorganization is not "retribution against the President..." No accountability for those Clinton policies and appointees that both encouraged a sloppy bureaucracy to disregard national security and punished those civil servants who defended national security. As William Safire had predicted the Rudman report was a "whitewash." This is a Clinton whitewash. It is a symphony of distracting smoke, mirrors, and noise.

On June 24, 1999 the House Governmental Relations Committee takes testimony from five whistleblowers. Rep. Curt Weldon, R-Pennsylvania, says he knew of ten others punished, fired, harassed, or demoted for speaking out about national security. The five civil servants claim retaliation for defending national security against Clinton China policy.

On October 24, 1997, the eve of the arrival of Chinese President Jiang Zemin to tour the U.S. in October 1997, Jon Fox of the Defense Special Weapons Agency was ordered — under direct threat of losing his job that day — to rewrite his own memo. A Pentagon arms control officer, Fox was ordered by the White House to say that the transfer of information about handling fissionable fuels is "not inimical (harmful) to the common defense or security of the United States." Fox drops his true view that it would "present real and substantial risks..."

Edward McCallum of DOE Security tells the Rudman Commission that the DOE has a "long history of suppression and reprisal" against those disclosing security breaches. Three days after McCallum talks to the Commission he is accused of a security breach, put on administrative leave, but is not pursued.

In early 1995 Robert Henson, a Los Alamos physicist, tips Trulock that nuclear warheads secrets may have been stolen. He is a long-time critic of lab security. In October 1995 DOE fires whistleblower Robert Henson in a staffing reduction, but hires 30 additional physicists — many of them Chinese nationals. Henson, 61, sues for age discrimination and gets his job back.

Michael Maloof. At the Pentagon's Defense Threat Agency, Michael Maloof opposes "wholesale" transfer of dual military and civilian technology to China because of its security threat to the U.S. He says he is "isolated, ignored and subject to political retribution" for his views. DOD spokesman Ken Bacon calls Maloof after he talks to the *New York Times* in 1998.

In 1994 a DOD senior export-control officer, Peter Leitner, disapproves a McDonnell-Douglas transfer of machine tools to a factory to China because it would help develop stealth weapons. He is ordered to change his recommendation. He refused, but it is exported anyway. Leitner says he lost normal promotions and bonuses. On October 19, 1999 U.S. Customs indicts the aircraft firm and its Communist Chinese cronies and employees.

Meanwhile back in the Senate, the forces of bipartisanship and cowardice can not be contained.

They blame the investigators

On June 28-29, 1999, the *New York Times* and Reuters report multiple sources and White House spokesman Jim Kennedy confirms that CIA Director John Deutsch briefed White House Chief of Staff Leon Panetta in July 1995 and NSC Advisor Tony Lake in November 1995 about Chinese nuclear thefts.

On August 5, 1999 the Senate Committee on

Governmental Affairs, chaired by Sen. Fred Thompson of Tennessee, releases a bipartisan report blaming the FBI and DOE for a bungled investigation, based on 30 hours of testimony. More astonishing, the Committee takes no position "on whether W-88 or other nuclear weapons information was in fact compromised, or by whose hand this may have occurred." The Senate report obsesses upon the two years it took to get a warrant on Lee's computer and blames the FBI rather than the Clinton appointees who had obstructed granting the routine warrant. Indeed, the Committee bought the position of DOJ that the FBI had blown the investigation despite evidence of obstruction and lies printed in every day's newspaper. Sen. Joseph Liberman, D-Connecticut, called it "a tragedy of errors." Janet Reno said she still didn't support a warrant on Lee.

On August 12, 1999 the coup de grace — the race card — is administered. A Committee of 100 Chinese-Americans says that prosecution of Lee would "unleash a virulent anti-Chinese frenzy in this country." [Hate crime watchers everywhere find no such frenzy anywhere.]

Robert Vrooman of DOE had already accused Trulock of racism, but his credibility is diminished. On August 12, 1999 Richardson chooses only Vrooman and two others out of 19 for public discipline of their poor performance — bureaucratic sloth — in the investigation. Clinton appointees Moler and Pena whose policies actively bred slack security and who punished those protecting national security get off easy. They are mentioned in a secret report of the DOE's Inspector General.

They are not publicly pilloried.

On August 24, 1999 Notra Trulock quits. He called the Inspector General's report a "whitewash" and objects to the race card. The original 12 suspects submitted to the FBI were three Chinese and nine Caucasians. The Chinese were a large portion of lab staff and they visited China frequently. The FBI, not Trulock, had focused on Lee. *Washington Post* reporters find three persons to say they believed Trulock was motivated by ethnicity. Trulock reminds everyone that Elizabeth Moler had gagged him before Congress so as not to hurt Clinton China policy. And that the DOE Inspector General had obstructed his investigation.

On September 22, 1999, the Senate votes overwhelmingly to reorganize the DOE bureaucracy to improve security. On the next day the FBI broadens its investigation to 500 suspects across the nation including private defense contractors. By November new suspicions focused upon one of the bomb assemblers — Sandia National Labs, Lockheed Martin, or the Navy.

Blame for racists, bureaucrats, investigators, and contractors — but not for the politicians who sold their nation's security for a few million in campaign cash.

Meanwhile the Clinton administration ships U-235 uranium to China for unknown uses, according to Charles Smith, *WorldNetDaily*.

Chapter 5

Chinese Shopping: American Military Technology

> *"The more you look into this business*
> *of the transfer of advanced,*
> *sophisticated technology to the*
> *Chinese military, which seems clearly*
> *for campaign contributions,*
> *the harder it is to stay away*
> *from words like 'Treason'."*
>
> Dick Armey,
> House majority leader, 1998

By the 1990s the Chinese had plans to buy or steal high technologies and plans to influence American elections. In 1993 Clinton met with Silicon Valley executives complaining about export controls on their trade with China. And in 1994 Clinton had Ron Brown and Hazel O'Leary run trade missions to China. By 1996 Clinton was running Dick Morris's plans to raise campaign cash. The Chinese and Clinton developed a serious and mutually beneficial working relationship.

Chinese military intelligence had a military technology-shopping list. According to *Insight* and others, this list included secret encryption, missile, satellite, nuclear and rocket technologies that could penetrate and destroy American defenses.

On a parallel political course, "...Chinese efforts in ...the 1996 elections were undertaken...in part by PRC intelligence agencies," according to the Thompson Report. The Cox Report noted, "Agents tied to the PRC's military industries ...illegally provided political contributions... to gain access to U.S. military and commercial technology."

In 1992 Clinton's future Pentagon team wrote for the National Academy of Sciences advocating loosening export controls on high technology. Clinton campaign manager Ron Brown turned the idea into a strategy to collect campaign contributions. In 1993 Clinton appointed the study's co-author William Perry deputy secretary of defense to loosen export control policies. And Clinton appointed Ron Brown, Secretary of the Department of Commerce, to advocate reductions of export controls for the corporate world. Before being sworn into office — in January 1993, Clinton met with Silicon Valley executives. They complained about President Bush's export controls on their high-tech products. Michael Armstrong, Chief Executive Officer of Hughes, reminded Clinton of his contributions to Clinton's campaign. Clinton contributor Armstrong strong-armed Clinton; "This will be public and political shortly."

The Thompson Report notes that John Huang's $45,000 in DNC contributions were timed very suspiciously. On Friday, September 24, 1993 — the day after Huang wrote the first two $15,000 checks to the DNC — Huang escorted Shen Jueren to the White House, where Shen met with Gore's chief of staff, Jack Quinn, and may have met with Gore. Shen's company, China Resources Holdings, is part of the PRC's Ministry of Foreign Trade and Economic Cooperation. Shen's company gathers intelligence for the People's Liberation Army of Communist China. China Resources made $100 million deals for its partner the Riady's Lippo Group, according to *Year of the Rat.*

In 1994 Commerce Brown and O'Leary led trade junkets to China, allegedly for campaign cash of $50,000 to $100,000 per seat. Accompanying them were the top fund- raisers for Clinton and the DNC — PLA pals Johnny Chung, John Huang, Charlie Trie, Loral chairman and Clinton contributor Bernard Schwartz. O'Leary met the head of China National Nuclear Corporation as she was loosening nuclear lab security in February 1995. Thefts from nuclear weapons labs accelerated.

Both the Loral and Hughes CEOs had close political associations with Clinton. Hughes CEO Michael Armstrong, a Clinton contributor, led Silicon Valley protests over export controls. Hughes "continually pushed the rules" to allow sharing of technical information with Chinese officials. The Cox Report: "In 1993 and 1995, Hughes failed to apply for...Department of State licenses...because Hughes knew that the Department...would be unlikely to grant the license... To this end, Hughes sought the approval of a Department of Commerce official...and claims to have sought the approval of a Department of Defense monitor...though Hughes knew that neither official was legally authorized to issue the required license."

Meanwhile, Loral President Bernard Schwartz wrote a $100,00 check in June 1994 to the DNC. Schwartz then joined the Ron Brown trade mission to China. According to Charles Smith, "President Clinton personally arranged for Loral CEO Bernard Schwartz to meet the Chinese vice Minister of the Commission on Science Technology and Industry for National Defense, COSTIND, a General Shen Rou-jun." In 1994 COSTIND's Gen. Shen completed deals with Bernard Schwartz of Loral to provide cheap Chinese rocket launches of expensive American satellites.

Clearly, the gift of missile guidance technologies from Loral and Hughes was helpful. Early rocket failures needed to be fixed, but security was a concern. The Commerce Department approved Hughes rocket launch assistance to the Chinese in 1995 while Armstrong was head of Clinton's export advisory council. It was "the most sweeping relaxation of export restrictions in U.S. history," stated the *New York Times*. There was more. According to the

Department of Defense, the Hughes and Loral analyses of Chinese rocket "failures" in January 1995 and in February 1996 radically improved the accuracy of Chinese missile guidance. (During 1992 a tougher Bush Pentagon, not Commerce, restricted the information shared after a similar rocket failure.)

Clinton export control waivers and slipshod security enabled Loral and Hughes to export improved rocket launch technology for satellites to China. Improved rocket launch techniques enhanced Chinese missile guidance greatly — pinpoint accuracy within yards of any target within 49 states. The Cox Report concludes that "U.S. national security was harmed."   Loral and Hughes improved "the guidance system of the PRC's Long March rocket" as did Clinton's waivers for Motorola satellite orbiting contracts. The Motorola technology doubles warhead firepower and allows independently maneuvering warheads to "penetrate enemy defenses."

In the fall of 1996, Gen. Ji Shengde was Chief of Chinese military intelligence. Gen. Ji ordered $300,000 transferred from PRC government-controlled accounts into Johnny Chung's bank accounts, according to Chung's testimony before a grand jury and corroborating U.S. and Hong Kong bank records.   Chung's key contact with Chinese military intelligence was through a woman. The lady was Lt. Col. Liu Chaoying, a Communist, high-tech spy, arms broker, military intelligence officer and daughter of Gen. Liu Huaqing, China's most senior PLA officer. Col. Liu gave Chung campaign contributions, met Clinton twice at California fundraisers — one giving her a photo with the President in 1996. Col. Liu is a graduate of China's top technical facility and its training institutions for Communist party leaders. She has been assistant to the president of two companies — China National Precision Machinery Import-Export Corporation and the China Great Wall Industries — which were cited by the United States in 1991 and 1993 for selling ballistic missiles to Pakistan. She is vice president of China Aerospace Industrial Holdings Ltd.

Liu's contributions to Clinton, laundered illegally through Chung, helped Loral get Clinton's a waiver to launch a satellite.

Coinciding with the arrival of Chinese and corporate campaign cash the Clinton administration gave wholesale waivers to export controls. From the White House down through the Departments of Commerce, State, Defense, and Energy, the Clintonistas ran rough-shod over every law, rule, and regulation concerning human rights and proliferation of nuclear, chemical, and biological weapons.

"State-owned or controlled companies — particularly those controlled by the PLA — are used increasingly as part of a Chinese network to acquire Western technology in the United States and other countries," noted *Jane's Defense Weekly*, December 17, 1997. The Cox report says that the Red Chinese government controls about 3,000 front companies having more than 10,000 agent-employees tasked to "collect" civilian technology with "dual" military uses. In July 1998 the Chinese government simply declared the end to such "private" companies. Many of these companies have ties with U.S. agencies regulating high technology exports. In 1998 Congress required the Department of Defense to list companies tied to the Chinese military operating in the U.S., but the Clinton administration had given no answer as of late September 1999 when Rep. Cox and nine others demanded it. Meanwhile under the Freedom of Information Act Charles Smith received an old PLA letter to Ron Brown listing Chinese companies interested in doing business in the U.S. In return, Brown provided the Chinese a catalogue of American high-tech companies wishing to do business with the Chinese military. Cozy. Congress not invited.

One man with a long shopping list was Wang Jun, head of China's principal arms trading company, Polytechnologies. Polytechnologies had multiple storefronts established in Los Angeles, China's "22nd province," according to detailed accounts in the *American Spectator*. Clinton pal "Charlie" Trie escorted Wang to a February 6, 1996, coffee with President Clinton and a meeting the same day with Commerce Secretary Ron Brown. Arms dealer Wang Jun was also introduced to persons on the New York Stock Exchange after his February 1996, meeting with Clinton. Perhaps Wang needed to finance some of those purchases.

The Chinese successfully stole nuclear technology but bought much of its other high technology with cash after Clinton's approval of waivers of existing trade laws. After directing cash into the Clinton campaign the Chinese and its high technology trading partners saw trade restrictions fall away.

Clinton waived export controls on dual use (militarily useful) technology. Some of these technologies are satellites, machine tools, rockets (missile guidance), supercomputers, aerospace machine tools, radiation proof microcircuits, lasers, cellular, encrypted, and fiber optic telecommunications.

Michael Maloof, chief of the Pentagon's Technology Security Agency, who oversees exports of dual-use (civilian and military) technology has waged a lonely fight to protect national security. In an internal memo subpoenaed by the Cox committee, Maloof says that the combination of supercomputers, satellite sales, and advanced telecommunications technology since 1994 "have provided the

Chinese with a nationwide encrypted command, control, communications, computers and intelligence (C4I) network that will serve it well into the next century." Maloof said, "Together they provide the PLA with a communications infrastructure that it could not have developed on its on." (*American Spectator*, May 1999). Maloof told the *New York Times* in late 1998 that the problem was "wholesale" decontrol of satellites, supercomputers, and stealth technology.

Clinton allowed COCOM, a regime of international export controls on militarily useful technology, to expire in March 1994 leaving many exports controls entirely up to national discretion. Similar expiration of the Export Administration in 1995 significantly reduced civil and criminal penalties for violations.

Clinton waived trade restrictions based on human rights violations arising out of the massacre of Tiananmen Square. He also certified that China had not proliferated weapons of mass destruction.

Clinton further loosened export controls on technology by moving approvals out of the security conscious Departments of Defense and State into the pro-trade Commerce Department. In particular, in 1992-1996, Clinton moved satellite licensing to Commerce — a decision greatly benefiting his Loral and Hughes contributors. (In 1998 Congress sent it back to the State Department and to Defense

Department participation.)

Clinton frequently overrode the expressed national security concerns of State, Defense, CIA, NSA, and the armed services. A few examples show the pattern.

In 1994 a DOD senior export-control officer, Peter Leitner, disapproves a McDonnell-Douglas transfer of the machine tools of a Columbus, Ohio, B-1 Bomber factory to CATIC a Chinese government company. Though the sale would help the Chinese develop stealth weapons, Leitner is ordered to change his recommendation. He refuses, but the Clinton administration allows the sale anyway. During the summer of 1999 in testimony before Congress, Peter Leitner reluctantly reports retaliation against him — loss of the regular promotions and bonuses received by his more compliant peers. On October 19, 1999 U.S. Customs indicts the aircraft firm and its Communist Chinese cronies and employees.

Secretary of Defense William Perry and companies tied to him twice override the objections of the National Security Agency to sales of encryption technologies to China. The NSA opposes Red Army receipt of both a factory to manufacture fiber optic cable and the installation of encrypted telephone switching equipment. Both protect the PLA from the electronic eavesdropping of the NSA. The NSA is silent after the sales are approved.

In 1996, the Clinton administration approves Hughes installation of 522 ground stations with ports for encryption for telecommunications satellites for the Chinese ground and rocket forces and air force.

Then 1998, according to a secret memo of March 12, 1998 by Gary Samore, a White House NSC aide, Clinton is willing to "...offer...expanded ... space cooperation, [and grant] blanket presidential waiver of Tiananmen Square sanctions to cover all commercial satellite launches." This assistance to Red China occurs against the recommendations of national security professionals.

Throughout 1999 in the midst of the nuclear espionage scandals, the Clinton Pentagon gives the top generals of the PLA a grand VIP tour of American nuclear labs and its military facilities, exercises, and training (procurement, logistics, electronic warfare, airlift, military medicine, nuclear labs). Such access will enhance Red China's military capabilities enormously. William Perry started the exchange program as "confidence building" for the Chinese (self esteem for tyrants). Gary Samore took a similar view in dismissing Chinese missile capabilities and advising Americans not to get excited. "[I]f our policy convinces China that we are a threat, ... China will ... significantly expand their strategic capability." Appeasing the dictators is an old illusion.

There is no reasonable doubt that Clinton cleared

the way for the sale and theft of America's highest technology to China. Red China is incorporating this technology into its war fighting and war winning capabilities.

Chapter 6

Chinese Shopping:
Super Computers

Early in 1993 John Podesta handles computer trade policy in the White House. John's brother, lobbyist Tony Podesta, has computer clients. On September 29, 1993 Clinton lifts major export controls on supercomputers. In May 1994 a group of computer companies, the Computer Systems Policy Project (CSPP) meets with Commerce Secretary Ron Brown, Treasury Secretary Robert Rubin, and trade aide Charlene Barshefsky to speed supercomputer sales to Russia and to China. Most of the companies are major "soft money" contributors. In August 1994 Tandem completes a deal to export $100 million in computers to PLA-owned Great Wall Industries (previously cited for missile sales to Pakistan and Iran) during a Ron Brown trade mission.

In November 1994, CSPP member and million-dollar donor Sanford Robertson writes President Clinton a letter thanking him for August trades mission to China. Robertson observes that Rubin has raised $100,000 for Sen. Dianne Feinstein from Silicon Valley contributors. The link between cash and trade deals is transparent in the Robertson note.

In May 1995 the private corporate CSPP asks

that export controls be eliminated for computers sold to civilian end users in Russia and China. CSPP argues further that controls on military users may also be eliminated "when there is greater certainty that neither [China nor Russia]...poses a threat to U.S. national security." The distinction between civilian and military users is a thinly disguised fiction to get around export controls since the Communist government — the Communist Army itself — controls the "civilian" Chinese companies.

Secret meetings are held in the White House. In October 1995, Clinton cuts controls on exports of computers. Gary Milhousin of the Project on Nuclear Arms Control calls it a payoff to Silicon Valley contributors. He also predicts that "civilian" computers would come into the hands of the military. They do.

In January 1996, the Commerce Department waives export licenses for militarily useful supercomputers (up to 7,000 MTOPS, a measure of the speed of computer calculations) to alleged "civilian" users. Such "civilian" computers are immediately diverted to PLA military research. By September of 1997, China is the largest owner of militarily useful US super computers. In December 1997, Commerce sanctions a supercomputer sale despite a Chinese denial of a U.S. inspection of "civilian" use.

On March 15, 1999, Rep. Cox reveals that Clinton's relaxed export restrictions gave China hundreds of high performance computers diverted into nuclear research. Such computers combined with access to Wen Ho Lee's millions of lines of "Legacy" code and the "Greenbook" (downloaded in the spring of 1998) could accelerate Chinese deployment of the seven stolen warhead designs. Indeed, *Softwar* reporter Charles Smith says a CSPP computer helped the PLA Air Force build a supersonic nuclear bomber.

After six months of Clinton delays the Cox Report is released in late May 1999: "[W]hile the PRC had virtually no High Performance [Super] Computers (HPCs) in 1996, the PRC had over 600 U.S.-origin HPCs at the end of 1998." Worse, those computers went directly into the hands of PRC organizations engaged in a wide range of military research and development — nuclear weapons, missiles, satellites, spacecraft, submarines, aircraft, command and control, communications, and microwave and laser sensors.

Fearing tightened export controls on computers after the Cox Report, Lew Platt of Hewlett-Packard and Andy Grove of Intel travel to Washington in June 1999 to lobby Congress. The next month most members of Congress defer to Clinton, dropping all export controls on computers up to 5,500 MTOPS and allowing sales to "civilian" companies up to 12,500 MTOPS. It really doesn't matter any more. The Communist Chinese already have more super computers than the Pentagon and DOE combined.

Beijing's parades of the DF-31, and the JL-2 missile tests appear to prove that the Chinese have shaved a decade off deployment of advanced, modern nuclear weapons.

Congress has a few days when it returns in January 2000 to reject the Clinton decontrol of super-computer exports.

There are many inherent conflicts of interest between preserving national security by not giving away secrets on the one hand and helping high-tech corporations make profits in trade with a hostile regime. Politicians looking for campaign cash from both the Chinese and their high technology traders compromise national security interests.

There is also an obvious and inherent conflict of interest facing those national security agencies charged with the responsibility to safeguard technology being urged to make high technology trade easier for campaign contributors — the Chinese and high technology companies. German firms selling poison gas and efficient crematoriums to Nazi death camps during the Forties do not today advertise those products and services. May we pray that our good free market friends in the Silicon Valley do not have such evils bothering their consciences in a decade or so.

Chapter 7

Clinton Propaganda and The Big Lie: Manipulating Media and Public Opinion

Never before in our nation's history has a topic of such importance to the future of the Republic, first received so little serious sustained news media attention and then been dismissed as a normal condition of international relations. Never before has a matter so threatening to the survival of the Republic been so downplayed in the media and in public opinion.

Our founding fathers took great pains to protect us from government control of the news. Clinton's manipulation of the media agenda and control of each day's news has only one comparable precedent — the Big Lie strategy of Adolf Hitler.

Clinton's spin has controlled the whole Chinagate story. The Chinese espionage, Clinton's favors for campaign cash, Clinton appeasement, and China's bellicosity and contempt create only one headline a week, if that, in a small scattering of newspapers.

With each new revelation of corruption, the Clinton administration strategy has been to deny, delay, dilute, and distract until the media and the public interest fades. For nearly four years the Clinton administration's NSC under Lake and Berger has successfully covered up Chinese thefts of nuclear warhead technology (controlled leaks during delays in declassifying Cox Report). Meanwhile its DOE continued relaxed security at nuclear laboratories, the Clinton administration punished those who objected (Trulock, McCallum, Henson), and kept the major spy suspect on the payroll.

Delays are obvious in the slow responses of the Clintonistas to requests for information — even court orders and congressional subpoenas. Denials are the continuous stream of lies on all matters big and small.

Creating events, timing releases or leaking incomplete information creates Clinton spin and headlines — those headlines distract from the bad news. For example, planned or not, the Monica distraction "about sex" and the partisan Democrat obstruction of impeachment and conviction – has now been replaced by one "Wag the Dog" foreign adventure after another. Each has driven shocking domestic matters of national security off the front page for three years. Clinton's bombing of an aspirin factory in Somalia and a cluster of tents in Afghanistan shifted to an air war in Serbia, then "peace" in Ireland, the Middle East, etc. Meanwhile, the Clinton Justice Department has ignored high crimes, prosecuted paperwork violations, and made soft plea bargains. These limp-wristed prosecutions have converted a Chinagate of high treason into a comic opera of inept Chinese-Americans not knowing what to do with their campaign checks. The real story — the treasonous use of Communist Chinese money to elect a Manchurian Candidate President — has been lost. Illegal Communist Chinese political contributions, bribery, corruption of our democratic process of self-government, treason are rarely mentioned. One hundred and twenty two persons take the Fifth Amendment, flee the country, and Chinagate is not news except to the followers of a few anti-Communist, "gadfly" organizations such as the United States Intelligence Council. Each little leaked incident or dribbled out fact distracts from learning the truth about Chinagate. The Clinton "spinmeisters" get results for their master.

Dilution is even more sophisticated. Reduce the impact of a bad story — the Cox Report — by delaying full release by claiming the report needs cautious declassification. The White House keeps newspaper stories classified. The President is too busy to discuss the report with Cox. So the full story is selectively dribbled out one drop at a time...W-88, neutron bomb, "lax security," computer data transfers...Many leaks are timed for holidays or late Fridays when the public is occupied with their private lives and actively avoids the news. That way bad news is lost or hardly noticed. Leak the least damaging version of the story. Leak the story to the back pages — political news given to a business news source. Leak story to a secondary source — AP, UPI, Salon — so that the elite newspapers will ignore what is not their exclusive. If it's not the *Times* (LA or NY) it's not fit to print.

The Big Lie has been astonishingly common with Bill Clinton. There are lots of Big Things to Big Lie about. Here are some examples from the Big Liar himself:

- **No corruption here.** "I don't believe you can find any evidence of the fact I changed government policy solely because of a contribution." Clinton, March 10, 1997.

- **No illegal money from China.** "We've spent $4 million and gave the (campaign-finance) task force millions of records and every shred of evidence, and they haven't found a thing."

- **Nobody told me.** "I can only say that America is a big country with a big government and occasionally things happen in this government that I don't know about."

- **Tough export controls.** Restrictions on exports to China "are tougher than those applied to any other major exporting country in the world."

- **No espionage exists.** "...the investigation has not yet determined for sure that espionage occurred. ...if anybody did in fact commit espionage, it is a bad thing, and we should take appropriate action."

• **Not on our watch.** "No one has reported to me that they suspect" [any espionage since his presidency began]. William Jefferson Clinton, Presidential press conference, March 19,1999.

• **Chinese innocent of proliferation.** "[I]f we hadn't been working with China, China would not have signed the Comprehensive Test Ban Treaty, the Chemical Weapons Convention; they would...not have refrained from transferring dangerous technology and weaponry to countries that we don't believe should get it."

• **We're investigating it.** "It is my understanding that the investigation has not yet determined for sure that espionage occurred."

• **No missile aimed at any child.** "For the first time since the dawn of the nuclear age, there is not a single solitary nuclear missile pointed at an American child tonight. Not one. Not a single one."

Clinton's lie about missile safety gives new meaning to the Big Lie — Clinton lied to the American people about their very survival.

And the Cox Report is delayed six months.

By mid-May 1999, the Cox Committee was still "negotiating" declassification with the Clintonistas, "like having the fox guard the chickens," according to *Insight* magazine and a Cox Committee source. Clinton delayed a meeting with Cox for ten weeks.

Forced finally to act, Clinton appointed former Sen. Warren Rudman as chairman and Rep. Jane Harman, as a member to the Foreign Intelligence Advisory Board to review operations at nuclear labs. Harman's prior law practice represented the People's Republic of China, requiring registration as a foreign agent. William Safire predicts a "whitewash." The Rudman report blames bureaucrats and the investigators not the traitors, not the obstructionists, and not the liars.

The Clinton NSC successfully and quietly quashes the Cox Report news of the neutron bomb theft, which the NSC had covered up for over two years. While Cox quietly tried to finish the top-secret work of his congressional committee by declassifying his secret report, from January through April the Clinton spin machine made selective releases. The leaks falsely stressed that there was little that was new, it was an "old story" and that China has been spying on the U.S. for two decades. Cox was described as "mad as hell." Clinton leaked the thefts of nuclear weapons designs attributing them all to Chinese spying and to lax security under Republican administrations.

The Clintonistas were lying and they knew it. They lied about what they knew and when they knew it. They lied about when the thefts occurred, when they were discovered, and what they did about them. They lied about security that did not exist and they lied about energetic investigations that were slothful. They lied by saying they wanted to get to the bottom of things, but denied warrants, refused documents, gagged witnesses, punished whistle blowers, and rewarded obstructionists.

From January until April 1999, the press downplayed the still classified Cox Report by dutifully running stories about Chinese espionage during the Reagan administration, about long-standing security lapses at the labs. Finally, the *New York Times* wrote, "until now, Clinton administration officials...have suggested that there is no evidence Chinese nuclear spying continued into the Clinton administration." The *Times* had finally detailed the 1995 theft, 1996 briefing, and the systematic cover-up of the neutron bomb secrets. It was an old story.

A dead story. Once told nobody cared anymore.

A compliant media and a cowardly Congress with notable exceptions left the many "Big Lies" unchallenged and unnoticed. The public lives in abysmal ignorance of greater dangers to our nation's survival.

In 1996 GOP presidential candidate Bob Dole, reluctant to make a big deal of presidential lying and the collapse of ethics and morality in the Clinton White House during the time he was Majority Leader, finally asked a good question, late in the campaign. "Where's the outrage?" Suddenly, the end in sight, he realized he was not catching up to the nimble Bill Clinton. "Where's the outrage" might be a better question to ask in 1999-2000. The mainstream news media scarcely yawns at the Clinton policy of helping Red China more effectively arm and aim nuclear missiles at our country.

In 1996 Clinton benefited from Red Chinese interference swinging American elections in favor of China's chosen "seeded" candidates. For nearly three years, the media has been Clinton lap-dog silent. In 1997 there was a virtual news blackout on the Thompson hearings. Begun in April, by mid-July 1997 not a single major network had televised the hearings of Sen. Fred Thompson. There was virtually nothing on the front pages of America's morning newspapers and a near total blackout by CBS, ABC and NBC evening news.

In 1998 the Cox hearings on sales and thefts of military technologies were mostly secret, but once the conclusions of the long classified report were released on a bi-partisan 9-0 vote, the Cox Report got one news day in the middle of the New Years holiday of 1999. And for six months — silence. Rep. Cox respected classified information and held his tongue. Clinton delayed meetings and declassification while his media spin operators and his political appointees in the departments of Energy, Commerce, Defense, CIA, Justice, etc., selectively dribbled out morsels of the content over six months.

Chapter 8

Collaborators:
Clinton and Red China

Bill Clinton's pursuit of Chinese cash and their interest in his political activities go back to the Mochtar and James Riady family in Arkansas during Clinton's early political career in 1979 and continued into the 1992 and 1996 Presidential elections. The Riadys are Indonesians of Chinese origin with loyalties to the People's Republic of China. The PRC gave the Riady's Lippo Enterprises concessions in China worth hundreds of millions of dollars. The Riady's Lippo Group is half-owned by the Beijing government.

The Riady family generously contributed to Clinton campaigns in Arkansas since 1979. By 1992, the Riadys were Clinton's largest contributor — more than any PAC, family, individual, or union.

The Riady ties to the Chinese — particularly Chinese intelligence — continue to this day. China Resources, headed by Chinese intelligence officer Liu, hold a controlling interest in Lippo's Hong Kong Chinese Bank. Recently the PRC pushed the McDonald's Corporation off their most profitable site in the world at Tiananmen Square giving the Riadys the site.

The Thompson report said, "[The tie] with a

Chinese intelligence agency...is based on mutual benefit, with the Riadys receiving...business opportunities in exchange for large sums of money and other help.

"James and Mochtar Riady have known President Clinton since the mid-1980s when they held a controlling interest in the Worthen Bank." Worthen Bank was central to the Whitewater land deal which led to successful convictions including the Governor of Arkansas. Are the Riadys part of a Red Chinese plan to "seed" candidates in the United States?

The Thompson report says, "The Riadys have visited Clinton in the White House...[T]he Riadys were heavy contributors to the DNC...They made...significant contributions...in...the 1992 elections;...Riady businesses, associates, and employees did likewise.   [T]hey were the employers of...Huang, whom they...place[ed] at...Commerce, then the DNC." Huang laundered PRC money into the Clinton campaign.

The Thompson Report continues, "In mid-1995, the President and his strategists decided that they needed to raise...many millions of dollars...above the permissible limits of the...campaign funding law if the President was...to be reelected. They devised a legal theory [of unlimited "soft" money to DNC, but not to the candidates] to support their needs and proceeded to raise...$44 million in excess of the

Presidential campaign spending limits. "Millions of dollars were raised in illegal contributions, much of it from foreign sources. When these abuses were discovered, the result was numerous Fifth Amendment claims, flights from the country, and stonewalling from the White House and the DNC."

Red Chinese Plan: Purchase a President

"[T]he PRC government fashioned a plan before the 1996 elections...its goal was to influence our political process...through...funding from Beijing"

U.S. Sen. Fred Thompson, R-Tennessee, chairman of the Senate Governmental Affairs Committee investigating illegal campaign fund-raising on July 8, 1997, soberly disclosed a China plan to influence the 1996 elections. Protecting intelligence sources and methods and not interfering with ongoing investigations, Thompson – like Rep. Cox 18 months later – was circumspect. In fact the CIA and FBI had authorized Thompson's statement and its disclosure.

The communist government of China had illegally poured "substantial sums of money" into U.S. political campaigns to "subvert our election process" and "buy access...in furtherance of Chinese...interests."

Hillary Clinton defends her husband (and her continued power) by claiming that there is a "vast right-wing conspiracy" responsible for his problems. Were Sen. Thompson's charges of Communist

Chinese campaign donations, all just a Right Wing rant? The liberal *Washington Post* star reporter Bob Woodward is not a member of the "vast right wing conspiracy."

Woodward's front-page story of July 13, 1997, reported,: "U.S. intelligence has established...$2 million was allocated by the Chinese government, of which at least $1 million was transferred to U.S. banks or to the Chinese Embassy..., [I]ntelligence... establishes that Beijing had the 'intent' to make illegal...contributions...

"Approved at the highest levels of the Beijing government, the plan was placed under the control of the Chinese Ministry of State Security, Beijing's...CIA."

How did the FBI know? "The FBI has electronic intercepts of conversations between government officials in Beijing and officials at the Chinese Embassy in Washington as early as 1995 calling for more than $2 million to be channeled into U.S. campaigns." explained *WorldNetDaily,* July 21, 1997.

Thompson's announcement was met with indifference and disbelief.

Here is the final Thompson Committee Report summary, with authors' commentary:

Strange coincidences

"The intelligence portion of the...investigation sought to determine whether the...the PRC ties were mere coincidence, or if the PRC was...behind...foreign political contributions.

Nobody was talking

"What the Committee learned was derived not from cooperative witnesses or the PRC, but from gathering information from our law enforcement and intelligence agencies and open sources, and piecing it together..."

Yet all the sources agreed

"The Committee determined from...law enforcement and intelligence agencies and open sources that the PRC government fashioned a plan before the 1996 elections ...to influence our political process ...through...funding from Beijing.

...[T]he PRC engaged in...more than simply "lobbying."...[M]ore than the original plan was being executed, and ...a variety of PRC entities were acting to influence U.S. elections."

Intelligence leaks blow the cover-up

On February 13, 1997, the *Washington Post* first reported a link between foreign campaign money and the PRC government.

"[S]everal DNC contributors and major fundraisers had ties to Beijing.

"A Justice Department investigation into improper political fund-raising activities has uncovered evidence that representatives of the People's Republic of China sought to direct contributions from foreign sources to the DNC before the 1996 presidential campaign." The Post observed that investigators "suspected a Chinese connection...because several DNC contributors and major fund-raisers had ties to Beijing," and identified, in particular, Yah Lin "Charlie" Trie and John Huang."...

Chinese lies and audio tapes

"The *New York Times* on March 13, 1997, wrote that "surreptitiously monitored" conversations between Chinese officials here and in Beijing "suggested that Beijing was prepared to take a drastic step: illegally funneling money to American politicians.

"*Time* reported in March that 'provocative' communications among Chinese officials picked up by American intelligence *monitoring* indicated that front companies for the Chinese government might try to funnel cash."

Boys from Beijing?

"Who might have directed this? According to the *Washington Post*, "top" Chinese officials approved plans "to attempt to buy influence with American politicians," and the plans continued through 1996 and to the present.

"Initial Indications were Consistent with What the Committee was Discovering About Foreign Money Being Funneled into the 1996 Elections."

Follow the money

"Early in the investigation, Committee staff discovered a number of money trails that led from the

DNC...back overseas...to Greater China. The trails wend their way from foreign countries through one bank account after another, ending up mainly in DNC coffers. Committee staff traced...trails backwards as far as the transaction...a wire transfer that brought into the United States funds...to make political contributions.

"Committee staff identified several instances of foreign money donations connected to six individuals with ties to the PRC. As noted below, John Huang, Maria Hsia, Ted Sioeng, and James and Mochtar Riady each have been associated in some way with the Government of China. The sixth, Yah Lin "Charlie" Trie, is a business partner of Ng Lap Seng, — AKA Mr. Wu — a Macao businessman with ...ties to the PRC. Trie escorted Wang Jun, head of China's principal arms trading company, Polytechnologies, to a February 6, 1996 coffee with President Clinton and a meeting the same day with Commerce Secretary Ron Brown. Nicholas Eftimiades, author of *Chinese Intelligence Operations,* writes that China Resources traditionally has a PRC military officer installed as a vice president. In 1993, China Resources purchased a 50% share of the Hong Kong Chinese Bank from the [Riady]Lippo Group.

"...in several cases Committee staff...identified a foreign account...as the source of a contribution to the DNC, they could not continue back to the actual trailhead ... since the Committee held no authority to compel production of foreign bank records. Hence, whether a contribution that entered the U.S. from an account in China, Hong Kong, Taiwan, Macao, Indonesia, or some other country was connected...to the PRC...could not be determined from...the records.

The Clinton-Chinese Conspiracy

"Campaign   Contributors'   PRC Connections...Information...reveals   close   ties between the PRC and ...the individuals who produced...foreign campaign contributions. And these individuals — Ted Sioeng, Maria Hsia, John Huang, and James and Mochtar Riady — interacted with one - another with some frequency. Their paths appear to have crossed most often when they were engaged in fund-raising...

"Evidence Emerges that the [PRC] Plan Was Implemented and...[More]...

"...the government of China may have allocated millions of dollars in 1996 alone to...influence our political processes during the...election cycle. Include:

• "A PRC government official devised a seeding strategy...to organize Chinese communities...to encourage them to promote persons from their communities to run in...state...elections...to develop ...candidates sympathetic to the PRC for future federal elections;

- "A U.S. agency received fragmentary reporting relating to China's efforts to influence the U.S. Presidential election;

- PRC officials discussed financing American elections through covert means;

- "A politically-sensitive transfer of funds may have occurred to a PRC-controlled account in the U.S.;

- "A PRC official...in a discussion...indicated an awareness that money placed in U.S. banks can be traced by U.S. law enforcement officials;

- " A PRC official encouraged Chinese-Americans to make political contributions and contact their Congressmen; and

- "Beijing was angered that its diplomatic officials in the U.S. failed to forewarn the Mainland about the burgeoning campaign finance scandal and that those officials were not aware of Chinese who went to Washington, D.C. for the purpose of lobbying or making political contributions.

The Facts

- "It is clear...illegal foreign contributions were made to the DNC and...these contributions were facilitated by individuals with extensive ties to the PRC.

- "The original sources of many of these contributions were bank accounts in the Greater China area.

- "It is also clear that well before the 1996 elections, officials at the highest levels of the Chinese government approved of efforts to increase the PRC's involvement in the U.S. political process.

• "Chinese efforts in connection with the 1996 elections were undertaken or orchestrated, at least in part, by PRC intelligence agencies."

PRC used overseas Chinese, U.S. citizens and residents.

"It is likely that the PRC used intermediaries. This is so because only U.S. citizens or legal permanent residents can contribute lawfully to political parties and campaigns. Moreover, the use of businesses and individuals as intermediaries is increasingly common among Chinese. It is also well established that the PRC wields influence over a wide range of entities and individuals, many of which conduct business directly with the PRC.

Chapter 9

Cover-up of Campaign Contributions

Brian Duffy and Bob Woodward, reported in the *Washington Post,* March 9, 1997, "...[T]he FBI...commenced a foreign counterintelligence probe...in 1996, briefing six Members of Congress regarding the Bureau's belief "that the government of China may try to make contributions to Members of Congress through Asian donors."

"The FBI also told the White House about the Chinese plan in June 1996, when FBI agents briefed two representatives of the National Security Council."

"The FBI briefings [of White House NSC] described illegal plans for the clandestine funding of American political campaigns..." In 1997, the Thompson Committee tried, but one hundred and twenty-two witnesses invoked the Fifth Amendment, demanded immunity, or fled the country, many to China, or refused to testify. At one point 18 critical witnesses fled the country, and another seventy-nine witnesses took the Fifth Amendment.

The Burton Committee. "Democrats on the House Governmental Reform Committee, as part of a strategy to discourage witnesses with damaging information on campaign finance abuses, sought to intimidate a key witness with limited knowledge of English and U.S. customs during a [September 29,]

1997 deposition, congressional records show." This according to Jerry Seper and Audrey Hudson of the *Washington Times* on August 19, 1999. Democrat lawyer Kenneth Ballen informed Manlin Foung that she would be facing TV cameras and 44 congressmen in testifying about a matter in which her brother, Charles Yah Lin Trie, faced criminal prosecution. Johnny Chung testified that he was coached to plead the Fifth Amendment before the House committee. Another 120 failed to cooperate.

Staff members of the Thompson Committee traveled to China, but Beijing stopped them cold. Jerry Seper of the *Washington Times* in February 1998 reported that the Chinese government was systematically blocking congressional investigators from traveling to Hong Kong and Beijing in pursuit of their suspects and their financial records.

The Chinese threatened arrests. The congressional investigators said that the Chinese Foreign Ministry in Beijing had issued standing orders — Beijing embassy officials in Washington were not to process visa requests for any congressional investigators seeking to visit China to probe the campaign-finance scandal. Chinese Embassy spokesman Yu Shu Ning denied that the visa applications had been rejected because of the investigation.

Strange, but the U.S. media had no such difficulties in interviewing their quarry in China. In a 1997 interview conducted by NBC News in Shanghai, Mr. Trie, once owner of a modest Little Rock restaurant, now owner of Daihatsu International Trading Corp., bragged that he could hide out in Asia for 10 years and planned not to return to the United States. Trie did return later for a soft plea bargain.

Rep. Dan Burton wrote to Secretary of State Madeleine K. Albright, saying "I find it outrageous that China would seek to block the U.S. Congress from official and legitimate business abroad."

After Burton's complaint Janet Reno joined the Chinese as a tag team against any Independent Counsel investigation and against cooperation with any and all Congressional Committees. Reno repeatedly rejected the private and public professional judgment of the men assigned to Chinagate, prosecutor Charles LaBella and FBI Director Louis Freeh. Both asked for a Special Prosecutor independent of the Clinton administration, but Reno refused.

And in April 1999 Premier Zhu Rongji mocked the United States saying he had billions of dollars to contribute. Why mess with Johnny Chung's $300,000 [from the head of Chinese military intelligence]? Zhu asked for "clues" from the United States so that he could investigate all these charges.

The Thompson Committee called secondary and tertiary witnesses. The Burton committee shut down. Back at the Thompson Committee the Democrats — aided and abetted by the Peoples Republic of China and the national news media — handled the few available witnesses dismissively.

Diverting attention from the substance,

Democratic senators shamelessly insisted that new campaign finance laws to solve a problem everybody was guilty of. Democrats chose to ignore the laws already on the books prohibiting foreign contributions, laundering, bribery, and treason (i.e. selling out the interests of your country for money). Sen. John Glenn would receive his payoff in a taxpayer subsidized free ride into space to relive his glory days as a young astronaut-celebrity attracted to cameras like a moth to warm light. The American public loves a fraud, particularly a self-advertising one with the "Right Stuff" and they all loved the shameless hokum of John Glenn, pathetic apologist for President Clinton and his Red Chinese keepers.

The Democrats on the Thompson committee wanted proof that Wu's money transfers to Trie actually came, not only from the Beijing government-owned Bank of China, but also from the government of China itself (Wu's employer in Beijing). Difficult to prove insofar as there was no direct testimony by Wu, Trie, or his assistant — all then hiding in China. The Democrats trusted uncooperative Red Chinese banks more than they did Swiss banks. After Trie returned and pled to minor paperwork violations the Clinton Justice Department was by July 1999 uninterested in any further testimony about several illegal contributions from Macao mobster Ng Lap Seng — AKA Mr. Wu.

Ordinarily there would be enormous public and news media pressure put on the Democratic Party and the President to come clean, to force the People's

Republic of China to stop serving as a "safe haven" for those called upon to testify.

But without press coverage and hence without public interest, the Thompson public hearings sputtered to a close. The staff worked quietly on a final report that received little public attention. We place generous excerpts of this report into the hands of thousands of Americans for the first time in this book.

Several Thompson associates — Edward Timperlake and William C. Triplett III — drafted the *Year of the Rat* published nearly a year after USIC's first monograph on the scandal, "What Red China Got for Its Money." An article with that exact title appeared in a recent *American Spectator* magazine. *The Washington Times* and *Insight* did excellent reporting, but most major U.S. news media continue to ignore illegal Chinese contributions and influence.

While Johnny Chung was talking, John Huang remained mute, invoking the Fifth Amendment before Larry Klayman's relentless questioning about the sale of trade missions to China. (Huang talked to the Burton committee in late 1999 only after a grant of immunity, but revealed nothing.) Jude Kearney, former Commerce official, claimed complete amnesia about his part in selecting participants for Ron Brown's flagship trade missions, allegedly from a prospect list of DNC contributors later found in Kearney's own office files.

By April 1999 the Chinese and Clinton were finally confronted with news of their nuclear and neutron espionage. Caught red-handed so to speak, Clinton still faithfully defended his benefactors.

"I can only say that America is a big country with a big government and occasionally things happen in this government that I don't know about," Clinton said. "So I think it's important that we continue the investigation and do our best to find out what happened and I asked for [Zhu's]...cooperation." Zhu followed up by saying that he would cooperate, provided the United States offered clues to help China.

Meanwhile in mid-February 1998, the *Investor's Business Daily* reported that Sen. Fred Thompson's committee would finally make public its report on fund-raising abuses by Democrats. The Congress had given up on getting to the bottom of the story.

[The Clinton Cover-up]:

Thompson report: "The FBI...told the White House about the Chinese plan in June 1996, when FBI agents briefed two representatives of the National Security Council. The FBI briefings described illegal plans for the clandestine funding of American political campaigns..." [Comment: Clearly, the Clinton administration knew about the plan, received the monies, and can hardly be a "victim" as they have so far successfully portrayed themselves. Editor.]

"A U.S. agency received fragmentary reporting relating to China's efforts to influence the U.S. Presidential election. The information is considered part of a criminal investigation and cannot be discussed with the Committee...

"The [Reno] Justice Department for the most part would not reveal matters that were the subject of its ongoing criminal investigation. While Justice's concern is understandable, it limits congressional oversight and makes it even more important that prosecutorial decisions be handled in a way that ensures public confidence." [Comment: The Reno Justice Department would appear to be obstructing justice and protecting the President. USIC editor].

During the summer of 1997 Laura Ingersoll, the Justice Department's "public integrity" section lawyer selected to head the campaign finance investigation told FBI agents "not to pursue any matter related to solicitation of funds for access to the President... That's the way the American political process works." FBI Agent Daniel Wehr told the Senate Committee on Governmental Affairs, "I was scandalized." FBI Agent Roberta Parker testified that "public integrity" attorney Ingersoll told agents the Justice Department "would not take into consideration" the president's legal defense fund and obstruction of the Senate's investigation. Four FBI agents said Ingersoll and her boss Lee Radek impeded and delayed the investigation.

Ingersoll refused a search warrant when Charlie Trie's assistant, Maria "Dia" Mapili, was observed destroying financial, business, and travel records. These include: a statement from the Red Chinese owned Bank of China in Macao; travel records for Ng Lap Seng — a Beijing employee in Macao in the

PRC — who had wired $1 million into Trie's bank account; and a Federal Express package showing 2 pounds of materials sent by the White House on May 5, 1997. In another instance Ingersoll refused to allow FBI agents to stop a man in a car driving away with legal boxes. Roberta Parker took 27 pages of notes on Ingersoll's actions. Ms. Parker surrendered her spiral-bound notebook, but it came back empty. The pages were apparently torn out — perhaps in Reno's X files. Ingersoll again refused a warrant after Trie's trash contained cancelled checks to the President's defense fund.

Four months later prosecutor Charles LaBella who replaced Ingersoll granted the search warrant. LaBella soon joined FBI director Freeh in seeking an independent investigator outside the Department of Justice. Janet Reno refused to appoint an independent prosecutor. Mapali later testified that Trie had ordered her to destroy records sought by the Senate. Reno gave Laura Ingersoll a special commendation for her work on the investigation.

By the summer of 1999, Fred Thompson says, "I would no longer rule out the possibility of obstruction of justice at the Justice Department." [blue sky or wet water. Editor USIC]. And calls for Reno's resignation meant nothing to her. "It is hard to overstate how little effect these attacks have on Janet Reno," said Walter Dellinger, her friend and former law partner. Clinton told Paul Sperry of *Investor's Business Daily,* "We've spent $4 million and gave the task force millions of records and every shred of evidence, and they haven't found a thing."

Orrin Hatch asked whether U.S. District Judge Norma Holloway Johnson had selected judges who were predisposed to "soft plea bargains." Hatch said "It looks as though they're covering these things up...Certainly, it looks like these plea bargains were deals, and we even worry about whether the judges were pre-selected so that they would give these soft plea bargains credibility."

In July 15, 1999 Justice Department Inspector General Michael Bromwich presented a 560-page top secret report on the fundraising scandal. He accused the FBI of holding back information from the Justice Department and said that Justice had "rushed to meet demands of Congress...engaged in a headlong dash to supply information..."

It was just a sloppy bureaucratic mess. Since long-range standards had been abandoned, information was of "dubious quality." The report showed, according to *Washington Post* reporter Roberto Suro that there was no "conclusive finding as to whether the alleged plot ever really existed." The Bromwich report was yet another Justice Department cover-up.

On July 27, 1999 Fox News reported that the Justice Department had since the fall of 1997 had Citibank records showing Chung receiving $300,000 from Chinese government officials, in particular a wire transfer from its Hong Kong office from Liu Chaoying. Liu is vice President of China Aerospace, satellite business partner with Loral and Hughes, and one of China's top spies. The Justice Department never bothered to pursue the bank records. Citibank was not cooperative according to both Justice and Rep. Burton.

On September 23, 1999 four FBI agents testified to the Justice Department impeding and delaying the investigation of Charlie Trie's destruction of records in 1997.

On August 6, 1999 Mark Middleton former White House aide with connections to Huang, Chung, and Trie refused to answer questions before the Burton Committee pleading the Fifth Amendment against self-incrimination.

From the Thompson report:

• "...the plan or parts of the plan and possibly-related PRC activities were implemented covertly in this country.

• "The individuals who facilitated the contributions have either elected to take the Fifth Amendment or flee the country.

• "Beijing has denied the Committee's request for assistance.

• "Moreover, after its hearings concluded...the Chinese leadership was pleased no PRC agencies have yet been implicated in the campaign finance scandal...

"In addition, there are indications that Chinese efforts in connection with the 1996 elections were undertaken or orchestrated, at least in part, by PRC intelligence agencies.

Chapter 10

The Cast of Characters: Bagmen

Here is the case for Bribery: Quid Pro Quo — cash for favors. And there's a large cast of characters:

Johnny Chung, a Taiwanese-born U.S. citizen and California businessman from Torrance residing in Artesia, was allegedly connected to murky business deals and was thought to be a petty "hustler" by NSC staff in the White House. Or so the Clinton character assassination and spin machine now says — after it was hustled or consented to be hustled by a paid agent of Chinese military intelligence. Shady or not, Johnny Chung was an unofficial delegate on Commerce Secretary Ron Brown's August-September, 1994 trade mission to China where Chung met with officers of the People's Liberation Army — probably his lady spy friend, Lt. Col. Liu Chaoing. Liu headed China Aerospace that launches satellites.

And during 1995 Chung alleges and the Thompson report confirms that a White House aide solicited him and he delivered a $50,000 check to Maggie Williams in the office of Hillary Clinton. Other records show that Chung was allowed to visit the White House over 50 times in the two years preceding the 1996 election, and raised more than $400,000 for the Democrats. Chung initially declined to speak to the Thompson committee investigators about the source of this money and how Red China might have been involved. For his $400,000 in donations, Johnny Chung appears to have purchased White House access — including meetings with the President — for himself and his Chinese associates. Chung, bagman for Red Chinese military intelligence, visited the White House 50 times. Any and all foreign contributions are illegal by law and every political activist knows that.

Through Chung, President Clinton allowed Hongye Zheng of the China Ocean Shipping Company (COSCO) to attend one of his Saturday morning radio broadcasts in 1996 before the election.

This was at least an "appearance of illegality" — enough to drive Newt Gingrich from office. The invitation came after Johnny Chung raised and transferred $400,000 into the coffers of the DNC.

Further, it was just days after COSCO adviser Hongye Zheng attended Clinton's Saturday morning radio broadcast, that Dorothy Robyn, member a Presidential economic advisory group, called City of Long Beach (CA) officials offering a Chinese deal to lease the Long Beach Naval Station to COSCO. The authors and the publishers of this book, the United States Intelligence Council, supported legislation in the Senate and House prohibiting the use of the Naval Station by COSCO. Despite acts of Congress, as we write the Port of Long Beach is swapping real estate with other tenants (Zim and Maersk) so COSCO will have "some needed room to grow," at Pier J according to port documents acquired by the authors. Yes, it's true; the Clinton White House initiated the COSCO deal.

COSCO is a lot more than a little Chinese shipping company. COSCO provides shipping services for the People's Liberation Army, smuggles assault rifles to gangs in Los Angeles, and purchased a Russian K3 nuclear attack submarine from Finland. COSCO has shipped arms to the Burmese tyranny and to Pakistan and nuclear materials to Iran. COSCO is quite simply the merchant marine for the Communist Chinese.

As it turns out, in the fall of 1996, some $300,000 came to Chung from Gen. Ji Shengde, chief of Chinese military intelligence for the People's Liberation Army. Once charged, Chung agreed to cooperate. Hundreds of pages of wiretaps reveal that Chinese intelligence tried to derail the Justice Department investigation. In particular Robert Luu in late spring of 1998 told Chung to protect Loral and Hughes. Blame the princelings — the irresponsible off-spring of Chinese leaders. Wiretaps suggest that President Jiang Zemin may have hatched the cover story and Luu: "Yes chairman Jiang agreed to handle it like this; the President over here [Clinton] also agreed." In addition to Chung's testimony, boxes of Chung's records — turned over to the Department of Justice in the fall of 1997 — and independently verified Citibank financial transactions in

Hong Kong and in Los Angeles corroborate this direct connection of official Chinese military intelligence to the Clinton contributions. The Justice Department apparently did not pursue the bank records. *The Los Angeles Times* reported on April 7, 1999 that "Chung's testimony has provided investigators the first, direct link between a senior Chinese government official and illicit foreign contributions that were funneled into Clinton's reelection effort."For reasons still unclear, "The [Thompson] Committee...received a detailed proffer from Johnny Chung and his attorney, as part of their request for immunity in exchange for...testimony after he invoked his Fifth Amendment privilege against self-incrimination. The Committee, however, declined to offer Chung immunity." Chung did choose to cooperate with the FBI and a grand jury.

After extensive FBI interviews from December 1997 to March 1998, Chung received threats to his livelihood and to his family and was moved into protective custody.

In December 1998 Judge Manual Real sentenced Chung to five years probation and 3,000 hours of community service. Judge Real criticized the DNC and the White House for claiming Chung had victimized them. Clinton and the DNC had been happy to take Chung's money along with Trie's, Riady's, Hsai's and others without ever asking from whence it came. We believe they knew from where it came and that it was illegal.

Rep. Dan Burton, R-Indiana, subpoenaed Johnny Chung to testify before the House Government Reform Committee. Burton wrote Attorney General Janet Reno who had for two years refused to appoint an independent counsel to investigate despite the recommendations of FBI Director Louis Freeh and the chief Justice Department investigator Charles La Bella. A clearly angry Burton wrote, "the American people have a right to the truth" about "Chinese government efforts to subvert our elections."

In early April 1999 the *New York Times* reported that Johnny Chung had testified that he was a bagman for the Chief of Chinese military intelligence, Gen. Ji Shengde, who had ordered $300,000 into Chung's bank account. Boxes of financial records and Hong Kong wire transfers corroborated the secret grand jury testimony of Chung. White House spokesman Jim Kennedy said the administration had no knowledge about the source of Mr. Chung's donations in 1996. U.S. District Judge Manual Real had commented on the DNCs alleged ignorance of the source of the same Chung funds, "If Mr. Fowler and Mr. Sullivan didn't know what was going on, they're two of the dumbest politicians I've ever seen." Judge Real demanded further that the DNC provide him with all DNC documentation on the matter. Real did not believe the DNC was a victim either. In March the Clinton Justice Department withdrew FBI protection despite Chung's claims of three attempts on his life.

In May 1999 Chung became the first person out of

100 who voluntarily appeared before Congress. Citibank in Hong Kong failed to respond to a Burton subpoena in July. In July Chung says the Justice Department "did not want to hear" new information he had offered. In late October 1999 Chung spoke before Larry Klayman's Judicial Watch. He asked why those familiar with campaign finance law were not being prosecuted.

John Huang was the focus of the Thompson Committee before its hearings began. "The goal was to understand why an executive at a small California bank (owned by a large Indonesian conglomerate), who raised money prolifically for the Democratic party and was rewarded with a political appointment at the Department of Commerce, was so often and well received by President Clinton and his staff."

John Huang was a former executive of the Lippo Group, an Indonesian conglomerate half-owned by the Red Chinese government in Beijing. The Lippo Group is headed by the Riadys, a wealthy family with extensive financial interests in China.

"The Riadys were also for many years generous supporters of President Clinton and the DNC."

The Riadys were known to have worked hand-in-glove with Red China.

Lippo paid Huang about $325,000 a year. According to the Thompson report: "The Riadys were Huang's patrons and supporters throughout his careers at Lippo and later at the Department of Commerce and the DNC." After Bill Clinton was elected president in 1992, Clinton asked that Huang be appointed deputy assistant secretary of the Commerce Department.

Lippo gave Huang a bonus check for $450,000. For what, might only be apparent later. Huang's future supervisor said that Huang was "totally unqualified." The Clinton administration had hired him anyway.

Huang appeared to come and go wherever he wanted while he was in the U.S. government. Huang, as civil servant on the payroll of the taxpayers, forbidden by law from raising money for campaigns, proceeded to raise funds for the DNC. The eager Huang illegally raised more than $100,000 for the Democrat party while on the public payroll at Commerce.

"In September 1993, Huang wrote three checks to the DNC, each in the amount of $15,000, each paid with foreign money. The checks were drawn on the accounts of three Lippo Group subsidiaries — Hip Hing Holdings, San Jose Holdings, and Toy Center Holdings. At the time the checks were written, all of the companies were losing money and operating in the red. Hearing testimony from a Huang coworker indicates the money for the three contribution checks came from Lippo accounts in Jakarta." (Testimony of Juliana Utomo, July 15, 1997.) The Huang checks in 1993 were paid with foreign money.

"Huang's $45,000 in DNC contributions was

made in close proximity to occasions when Huang may have arranged for Vice President Gore to meet Shen Jueren, the head of a commercial enterprise wholly owned and operated by the PRC's Ministry of Foreign Trade and Economic Cooperation. Called China Resources Holdings, Shen Juaren's company has been identified as a PRC intelligence-gathering operation; one with reported ties to the People's Liberation Army," said the Thompson report.

On Friday, September 24, 1993 — the day after Huang wrote the first two $15,000 checks to the DNC — Huang escorted Shen Jueren to the White House, where Shen met with Gore's chief of staff, Jack Quinn, and may have met with Gore as well. The following Monday, September 27, 1993, Huang wrote another $15,000 check to the DNC. On the same day, at a Santa Monica event organized by Huang and Maria Hsia, Shen Jueren may have met again with Vice President Gore.

At Commerce, Huang's boss later claimed he wanted Huang "walled off" from any matters dealing with China or even Asia. That did not happen. Indeed, Huang received a top-secret clearance before his first day of work at Commerce and acquired access to many documents on China. Yet Huang attended 109 classified CIA and other security and intelligence briefings and as often as two or three times a week, Huang crossed the street to make phone calls and pick up faxes at Stephens Inc., an Arkansas investment firm with ties to the Lippo group. A former secretary observed his visits. Democratic Sen. Joseph Lieberman of Connecticut concluded, "These visits I find very curious." At Commerce for 18 months, Huang placed more than 400 telephone calls to representatives of Lippo and made frequent visits to the Chinese Embassy. The Thompson report said that Huang "may possibly have had a direct financial relationship with the PRC government."

Later — September 1997 — the House Government Affairs Committee was investigating whether Huang gave sensitive economic data to the Riadys. "Insider information, going through the Riadys, perhaps to the People's Republic of China...would enable the Chinese government to prepare themselves for trade negotiations [and] put the United States at a serious disadvantage," Rep. Dan Bennett said.

None of this much bothered Huang's superiors. "In fact, James Riady attended a small meeting in the Oval Office on September 13, 1995, at which President Clinton was asked if he would help Huang move from Commerce to the DNC," says the Thompson report.

After a DNC interview with Harold Ickes at the White House on October 2, 1995, at Ickes request, Huang claims to have raised $7,000 for Jesse Jackson Jr. while still a Commerce employee.

"President Clinton acceded to the request, and by the end of the year, Huang became the DNC's vice-chairman of finance, a position created especially for him," according to the Thompson report. Honoring the Riady request, Bill Clinton recommended Huang to a top fund-raising post for the Democratic National Committee before the 1996 elections.

While dialing for dollars at the DNC, Huang continued his relations with Lippo and the government of the Democratic People's Republic of China. Huang raised some $1.6 million for the Democrats, much of it apparently from illegal, foreign sources. Over time Huang would raise $3 million for the DNC.

"In 1996, John Huang solicited some $3.4 million in contributions to the DNC. Nearly half this amount has been returned as the contributions were determined by the DNC to have been made with actual or suspected foreign funds," says Thompson report.

Larry Klayman of Judicial Watch in his own pursuit of Former Commerce Secretary Ron Brown for possible sale of corporate seats on trade missions was one of the first to run across John Huang. Klayman was scheduled to depose Huang in April and May 1999 seeking to confirm other testimony and suspicions that Clinton's Commerce Department sold trade mission seats including those of a mission to China in 1994. Klayman has asked Huang whether China used participants as espionage targets and whether Huang passed classified information to the Chinese. Huang has refused to answer, taking the Fifth Amendment.

"The Committee's interest was further piqued by the fact that to date, the DNC has returned half of the money Huang raised in 1996. The DNC has been unable to verify that these funds derived from a legal, domestic source. The Committee has examined in detail Huang's activities at Lippo, Commerce, and the DNC. A single piece of unverified information shared with the Committee indicates that Huang himself may possibly have had a direct financial relationship with the PRC government." The Thompson committee may be referring to the $100,000 that John Huang wired Webster Hubbell from the Hong Kong Chinese Bank, according to the *Year of the Rat.* (Charges against Hubbell were reinstated in May 1999.) Or perhaps the Committee was referring to John Huang's overheard conversation about political contributions with a Chinese official at the Los Angeles consulate of the PRC (*New York Times,* December 15, 1998).

Haung cooperated with Justice providing 20 sessions. He was eventually charged with two illegal contributions — $2,000 to Michael Woo and $5,000 to the California Victory Fund and Sen. Diane Feinstein. Ty Cobb, Huang's lawyer said that Huang "was not the main leader." Huang has been sentenced to probation for conspiring to violate federal fund-raising laws.

Several Republicans in Congress have accused

Mr. Huang of "economic espionage." Rep. Bennett said, "For years, he was the primary political agent in America for the Riady family — a group of Chinese billionaires whose business headquarters are in Indonesia."

There can be little doubt that Huang's contributions influenced U.S. policy toward both Indonesia and China.

On August 13, 1999 District Judge Richard Paez sentenced Huang to one year's probation and no jail time, a $10,000 fine and 500 hours community service. The judge urged cooperation with Congress, but Reno denied immunity to Huang for Congressional testimony since he might possibly be called in an espionage case.

Yah Lin "Charlie" Trie, a Little Rock restaurateur and 14-year friend of Bill Clinton, at Clinton's request became a DNC finance board director.

Mr. Trie's DNC trusteeship entitled him to special privileges, including 23 known White House visits.

The Thompson Committee reports:

"Yah Lin 'Charlie' Trie also solicited large amounts of foreign money. In Trie's case, the cause was the Presidential Legal Expense Trust; set up to help satisfy the legal bills incurred by President and Mrs. Clinton... In March 1994, Trie brought nearly half a million dollars in small-denomination checks and money orders to the law office administering the Trust. Followers of a Buddhist Sect called Suma

Ching Hai wrote the checks and money orders. Trie claimed that many of the followers were reimbursed in the amount of their contributions. Ultimately, the reimbursement money came from accounts in Taiwan and Cambodia"

On February 6, 1996, Trie had a meeting with Ron Brown and arms dealer Wang Jun the same day the dealer had a White House coffee with President Clinton. Trie arranged Clinton's meeting with Wang, head of the arms smuggling Polytechnologies. Wang's visit to the White House was previously reported, and Clinton has said it was "inappropriate." Clinton himself granted Polytechnologies a waiver to bring 100,000 semi-automatic weapons for sale in the U.S. The February 1996 meeting between Brown and Wang — given his arms dealing for the PLA — made Wang more than merely an illegal foreign contributor.

The New York Times claimed that Trie had asked Beijing for $1 million for his political activities. The $1 million wired from Mr. Wu in Macao may indeed have come from the Chinese government

The Thompson Committee discovered that Wu, AKA Ng Lap Seng, an advisor to the Chinese government, transferred $1.4 million from foreign banks in 41 separate wire transfers to Charlie Trie. In 1996 the Beijing controlled Bank of China sent Trie funds in chunks of $50,000 and $100,000.

Ng Lap Seng, (AKA Mr. Wu) apparently bought himself 10 trips to the White House — one for dinner with the President of the United States.

"None of the aforementioned individuals would speak to the [Thompson] Committee about their fund-raising activities. Sioeng left the country soon after the campaign finance scandal broke. The Riadys likewise have stayed out of the United States, and declined to meet with Committee staff working in Indonesia. Huang and Hsia [below] have remained in this country but have both asserted their Fifth Amendment privilege against self-incrimination," says the Thompson report. Trie and his assistant trashed records that the Thompson Committee sought while the FBI futilely fought for four months to get search warrants approved by Laura Ingersoll. Charles LaBella approved them.

FBI agent Jerry Campane confirmed that Yah Lin "Charlie" Trie laundered foreign money that may have been from the Communist Chinese government. Yue Chu, whose husband worked for Trie's business partner, Ng Lap Seng in Beijing, testified that she wrote checks to the Democratic National Committee and was immediately reimbursed by her husband's Beijing boss.

Trie fled, but returned to be arrested. After a long-delay, the Justice Department indicted Trie on January 28, 1998, on 15 counts, including conspiracy to defraud the DNC and the United States. Trie conspired to purchase access to officials via donations to the DNC. The alleged victim in these cases being the DNC.

Trie returned from China to surrender February 3, 1998, to FBI agents at Washington Dulles International Airport and pled innocent to all charges on February 5, 1998. Mr. Trie pleaded not guilty to conspiring to buy political influence through the illegal diversion of campaign cash to the Democratic National Committee.

Trie's attorney, Reid H. Weingarten, told reporters his client had become a victim of congressional investigators who wanted to portray Mr. Trie as a spy. "He has never served as a spy for a foreign country. He never intended to corrupt the American political system," Mr. Weingarten said. The lawyer did not indicate whether he thought that his client, like Mrs. Clinton's husband, is also the victim of a "vast rightwing conspiracy." *Associated Press* reported April 25, 1999, "Trie, longtime friend of Clinton and a former Little Rock restaurateur, is scheduled to go on trial May 17 [before U.S. District Judge George Howard Jr.] on charges he made and arranged illegal contributions to the Democratic National Committee to buy access to Clinton and other top officials.

The indictment also claims Trie obstructed justice by ordering an employee to destroy documents subpoenaed in 1997 by a federal grand jury and by the Senate Governmental Affairs Committee..."

A judge threw out most of the charges, but by May the U.S. Court of Appeals was expected to reinstate the charges. On May 22, 1999 facing reinstatement of most charges Trie pled guilty to two fund-raising charges and agreed to cooperate with further Justice Department investigations. Instead of six years in federal prison and a $350,000 fine Trie received three years probation.

QUID. Trie delivered $664,000 to Clinton's legal defense fund. Charlie Trie once dumped open a paper bag full of checks on a desk. The legal expense money was finally returned and its original receipt initially covered up. Returned also was another $600,000 for a combined total of $1.2 million that Trie raised for Clinton.

PRO QUO. The President then named Trie to a trade commission post, which Trie used to assist Communist China, where he first fled to avoid subpoenas from Congress.

Trie's money and that of his Chinese friends got what they paid for. Ng Lapseng, AKA "Mr. Wu," contributor of $80,000 from the Bank of China in Macao, got his ticket punched at the White House, early and often. Wu visited the White House at least 10 times between 1994 and 1996; Antonio Pan, Trie and Huang associate, visited the White House eight times. Trie at least 23 times. Clinton appointed Trie to the Commission on United States-Pacific Trade where Trie set up a secret coffee between Clinton and Wang Jun, China's primary arms dealer.

As Chung put it, he wanted "to come visit the White House... to buy a ticket to pass the gate." Proof that Ng, AKA Wu, thought the place was for sale. Wu is a member of an entity providing economic advice to the Communist Party and the central government in Beijing. Wu was also a business associate of Wang Jun, chairman of CITIC, a large Chinese "company" owned by the government — China's arms dealer. Why has there been no outrage that White House access was sold not for petty special interests but instead to a hostile foreign power? "Where is the outrage?"

In videotapes made available in October 1997, after six months of White House delays, Clinton can be seen amicably socializing with some of the above characters — among them John Huang, Yah Lin "Charlie" Trie, Pauline Kanchanalak, James Riady and Johnny Chung. The tapes show at least two instances in which Clinton acknowledged that some of the guests at a fund-raising event were from foreign countries [and thus, illegal contributors]. At an Asian American fund-raising event

February 19, 1996, at the Hay-Adams, Clinton refers to "my good friend John Huang," and thanks him for putting on the dinner. "I have known John Huang a very long time."

At a May 13 dinner, Clinton thanked Huang and then turned his attention to former Little Rock restaurateur Trie, who was seated next to the president; "It's been 20 years since I had my first meal with Charlie Trie..."

Also featured on the videotapes was Johnny Chung, who escorted six Chinese executives from state-owned and "private" businesses (ie. a "private Communist" business is an oxymoron) to the Oval Office.

September 10, 1994,...a lengthy but inaudible discussion of Clinton with Riady and Huang. At a radio address on June 24, 1994, Riady was introduced to the president. At a fund-raiser on July 30, 1996, at the Jefferson Hotel, foreign nationals' Riady and Taiwan insurance billionaire Eugene Wu attended. Clinton talked about his decision to send carriers into the Taiwan Straits after Beijing test-fired missiles near the breakaway island.

They paid their money; they got their access.

What else have they gotten?

Congressman Gerald Solomon asked: "Is this what China is getting in return for its big donations to Clinton and the Democrat National Committee campaign coffees?"

Chapter 11

Al Gore and Friends

As leaked to Bob Woodward in the *Washington Post,* the final Thompson report said: "...Hsia has been an agent of the Chinese government, which she has acted knowingly in support of it, and that she has attempted to conceal her relationship with the Chinese government...Hsia has worked in direct support of a PRC diplomatic post in the U.S. ...Hsia first met Vice President Gore in the late 1980s, and organized a trip he attended to Taiwan in 1989. She has raised money for the Democratic Senatorial Congressional Committee ("DSCC"), and lobbied to have DSCC contributions earmarked for then-Senators Gore and Simon. On September 27 1993, she attended the Santa Monica, California event with John Huang where Shen Jueren may have met Vice President Gore. In connection with that meeting, Hsia contributed $5,000 in money illegally laundered through the Hsi Lai Temple.

"Hsia has a long-standing relationship with the Hsi Lai temple. She, with Huang, organized the April 1996 fund-raiser held there and attended by Vice President Gore, and laundered thousands of dollars illegally through temple clerics in connection with the event.

"The Committee has identified over $130,000 in political contributions illegally laundered through

temple monastics at Hsia's direction...Hsia worked
with Ted Sioeng and John Huang to solicit contributions from Chinese nationals in the United States
and abroad...

"Hsia and Huang...worked together to identify
non-U.S. citizens overseas who might contribute
money..."

The Thompson report describes Gore meeting
another person connected to China Resources, a
known front for Chinese intelligence, agent for the
Chinese in Panama, and generous Riady business
partner — Li Ka-shing. "Were such alleged intelligence reports to be true, Hsia's long relationship to
the vice president of the United States would raise
grave new questions about the extent to which
Chinese intelligence operations have been able to
influence U.S. politics during the Clinton administration," says the Thompson report.

The final Thompson report says: "Maria Hsia
was involved in soliciting contributions to the DNC
that were laundered through several Buddhist
monks and may have derived from foreign sources.
Once the figures had been tallied for the April 29,
1996, Hsi Lai Temple fund-raiser attended by Vice
President Gore, it became apparent that the event
had not generated the level of contributions expected by the DNC."

DNC Finance Director Richard Sullivan asked
Huang to "get some California money in." Huang
turned to Maria Hsia, who engineered a scheme

whereby some $55,000 was contributed to the DNC by temple monastics who, in turn, were reimbursed out of the Temple's general expense account. The source of the Temple's money is believed to be Buddhist devotees and may derive from overseas. (Testimony of Juliana Utomo, July 15, 1997.)

Investor's Business Daily found that Vice President Al Gore had longtime links to Maria Hsia going back to 1988 and an early 1989 trade trip that Gore, Hsia and others took to Taiwan, Indonesia and Hong Kong. Among others apparently along for the plane ride was John Huang, working for Lippo Bank.

Gore's relationship to Hsia was hardly casual — she helped him write his much-ballyhooed book on the environment. Gore's then chief of staff Peter Knight wrote a letter to Hsia, saying: "The materials you got for Al's book on the environment were perfect. ... He would have been lost without your efforts because the chapter on religion and the environment was integral to his work." As reported in the *Wall Street Journal* in mid-February, 1998 the Justice Department indicted Ms. Maria Hsia, 47 years old, before a federal grand jury. Hsia was charged with one count of conspiring to defraud the U.S. by securing contributions for the Clinton-Gore campaign from non-U.S. citizens and foreign entities, in violation of federal election laws.

The grand jury also charged Ms. Hsia with five counts of making false statements to the Federal

Election Commission. The Buddhist temple had tried to cover up the tangle of contributions and cash reimbursements by altering canceled checks and by destroying documents.

Attorney General Janet Reno declared that Ms. Hsia's indictment was "another step forward." On September 10, 1998, U.S. District Judge Paul Friedman dismissed five of the six charges saying it was "Alice in Wonderland" logic that Hsia be blamed for false campaign filings to the Federal Elections Commission. False records, false names, false corporate status, false amounts were not enough for the Judge. It was an odd decision. Anyone with Hsia's experience raising funds for candidates over several election cycles knows the rules about who can legally give. They know fraud and money laundering are illegal. The judge's ruling was passing strange. So too thought the unanimous three-judge panel of the U.S. Court of Appeals for the District of Columbia which on May 19, 1999 overturned Judge Friedman and reinstated five of six criminal charges for giving phony names for contributors to the Federal Elections Commission. Two of the three judges were Clinton appointees.

Will Congress Act?

From its oversight of our Justice System, to its ability to supervise the national defense and security interests of our country, to its ability to demand answers to questions from the Executive Branch, the questions raised in this book, need to be answered by Congress.

We pray our elected representatives will do their duty under the Constitution as a co-equal branch of our national government. The power to conduct hearings, subpoena witnesses, hold witnesses in contempt, the power of the purse, the power to remove executive branch officials who break the law or fail to cooperate. These powers granted to Congress ought to be used. Hopefully, there are not yet enough Senators and Congressmen tainted by Red Chinese cash to thwart justice. We hope and pray that the American people will force Congress to ask why Bill Clinton is the China Doll, and how he became Red China's favorite President.

How You Can Help USIC

Dr. Roger Canfield and Richard A. Delgaudio are available as speakers on the subject of this book. While neither require an honorarium, travel expenses would be appreciated. Both are also available for radio talk show interviews and appreciate the help of our readers and friends in securing such engagements. To order additional copies of this book please complete the order form below and mail it to:

Dr. Roger Canfield & Richard A. Delgaudio
U.S. Intelligence Council, Office of the Chairman
10560 Main St., Suite 217 • Fairfax, VA 22030

━━━ *"China Doll" Order Form* ━━━

❏ Single copy, $4.95   ❏ Two copies, $8   ❏ Three Copies, $11

(A 40% discount is available to booksellers and for orders of 100 books, plus $20 shipping. Quantity_____ , $ _____ enclosed.)

❏ "What Red China Got for its Money," originally published in 1997, reprinted in 2000 with a new Afterword, by Dr. Roger Canfield, $2 or free with any book order

❏ Donation enclosed to support the ongoing work of the U.S. Intelligence Council $ _____

Please add a $2 shipping and handling fee to your order total
Total amount enclosed $_____

Please make your check payable to USIC. Thank you.

Name_____

Address_____

City/State/Zip_____